Contents

BURRITO PIE

Servings: 16 | Prep: 30m | Cooks: 30m | Total: 1h

NUTRITION FACTS

Calories: 432 | Carbohydrates: 33.3g | Fat: 23.9g | Protein: 19.8g | Cholesterol: 68mg

INGREDIENTS

- 2 pounds ground beef
- 1 (10 ounce) can diced tomatoes with green chile peppers
- 1 onion, chopped
- 1 (16 ounce) jar taco sauce
- 2 teaspoons minced garlic
- 2 (16 ounce) cans refried beans
- 1 (2 ounce) can black olives, sliced
- 12 (8 inch) flour tortillas
- 1 (4 ounce) can diced green chili peppers
- 9 ounces shredded Colby cheese

DIRECTIONS

1. Preheat oven to 350 degrees F (175 degrees C).
2. In a large skillet over medium heat, saute the ground beef for 5 minutes. Add the onion and garlic, and saute for 5 more minutes. Drain any excess fat, if desired. Mix in the olives, green chile peppers, tomatoes with green chile peppers, taco sauce and refried beans. Stir mixture thoroughly, reduce heat to low, and let simmer for 15 to 20 minutes.
3. Spread a thin layer of the meat mixture in the bottom of a 4 quart casserole dish. Cover with a layer of tortillas followed by more meat mixture, then a layer of cheese. Repeat tortilla, meat, cheese pattern until all the tortillas are used, topping off with a layer of meat mixture and cheese.
4. Bake for 20 to 30 minutes in the preheated oven, or until cheese is slightly brown and bubbly.

ANGELA'S AWESOME ENCHILADAS

Servings: 8 | Prep: 45m | Cooks: 1h | Total: 1h45m

NUTRITION FACTS

Calories: 709 | Carbohydrates: 52.5g | Fat: 36.3g | Protein: 42.2g | Cholesterol: 126mg

INGREDIENTS

- 2 pounds skinless, boneless chicken breast meat - cut into chunks
- 1 bunch green onions, chopped, divided
- 1 (10.75 ounce) can condensed cream of chicken soup

* 1 cup water
* 1 1/4 cups sour cream
* 1 teaspoon lime juice
* 1/4 teaspoon chili powder
* 1/2 teaspoon onion powder
* 1 tablespoon butter
* 1/2 teaspoon garlic powder
* 1 small onion, chopped
* 5 (12 inch) flour tortillas
* 1 (4 ounce) can chopped green chilies, drained
* 3 cups Cheddar cheese, shredded, divided
* 1 (1.25 ounce) package mild taco seasoning mix
* 1 (10 ounce) can enchilada sauce
* 1 (6 ounce) can sliced black olives

DIRECTIONS

1. Place the chicken in a large pot and add water to cover. Bring to a boil over high heat, then reduce the heat to medium-low, cover, and simmer until the chicken pieces are no longer pink, about 10 minutes. Shred chicken by placing two forks back to back and pulling meat apart. Set the shredded chicken aside. Meanwhile, combine the cream of chicken soup, sour cream, and chili powder in a saucepan. Bring to a simmer over low heat, stirring occasionally, then turn off the heat and cover to keep warm.
2. Heat the butter in a skillet over medium heat. Stir in the onion; cook and stir until the onion has softened and turned translucent, about 5 minutes. Add the shredded chicken, chopped green chilies, taco seasoning, half of the bunch of chopped green onion, and water. Allow to simmer for 10 minutes. Stir in the lime juice, onion powder, and garlic powder; simmer for an additional 10 minutes.
3. Preheat an oven to 350 degrees F (175 degrees C). Stir 1 cup of the soup mixture into the skillet with the chicken mixture. Spread the remaining soup mixture on the bottom of a 9x13 inch baking dish.
4. Fill each tortilla with chicken mixture. Sprinkle Cheddar cheese over the chicken filling before folding the tortillas, reserving half of the shredded cheese for topping the enchiladas. Fold tortillas over the filling and place seam-side down in the prepared pan.
5. Pour enchilada sauce evenly over the enchiladas. Cover with the remaining 1 1/2 cups of Cheddar cheese. Sprinkle the reserved chopped green onions and the sliced olives on top of the cheese. Bake in the preheated oven until filling is heated through and the cheese is melted and bubbling, about 25 minutes.

CHICKEN ENCHILADAS

Servings: 8 | Prep: 30m | Cooks: 30m | Total: 1h30m | Additional: 30m

NUTRITION FACTS

Calories: 498 | Carbohydrates: 49.7g | Fat: 15.9g | Protein: 26.7g | Cholesterol: 72mg

INGREDIENTS

- 4 skinless, boneless chicken breast halves
- 1 (15 ounce) can tomato sauce
- 1 onion, chopped
- 1/2 cup water
- 1/2 pint sour cream
- 1 tablespoon chili powder
- 1 cup shredded Cheddar cheese
- 1/3 cup chopped green bell pepper
- 1 tablespoon dried parsley
- 1 clove garlic, minced
- 1/2 teaspoon dried oregano
- 8 (10 inch) flour tortillas
- 1/2 teaspoon ground black pepper
- 1 (12 ounce) jar taco sauce
- 1/2 teaspoon salt (optional)
- 3/4 cup shredded Cheddar cheese

DIRECTIONS

1. Preheat oven to 350 degrees F (175 degrees C).
2. In a medium, non-stick skillet over medium heat, cook chicken until no longer pink and juices run clear. Drain excess fat. Cube the chicken and return it to the skillet. Add the onion, sour cream, Cheddar cheese, parsley, oregano and ground black pepper. Heat until cheese melts. Stir in salt, tomato sauce, water, chili powder, green pepper and garlic
3. Roll even amounts of the mixture in the tortillas. Arrange in a 9x13 inch baking dish. Cover with taco sauce and 3/4 cup Cheddar cheese. Bake uncovered in the preheated oven 20 minutes. Cool 10 minutes before serving.

CHICKEN FLORENTINE CASSEROLE
Servings: 4 | Prep: 25m | Cooks: 25m | Total: 50m

NUTRITION FACTS

Calories: 647 | Carbohydrates: 17.6g | Fat: 38g | Protein: 61.6g | Cholesterol: 168mg

INGREDIENTS

- 4 skinless, boneless chicken breast halves
- 1/2 cup half-and-half
- 1/4 cup butter

- 1/2 cup grated Parmesan cheese
- 3 teaspoons minced garlic
- 2 (13.5 ounce) cans spinach, drained
- 1 tablespoon lemon juice
- 4 ounces fresh mushrooms, sliced
- 1 (10.75 ounce) can condensed cream of mushroom soup
- 2/3 cup bacon bits
- 1 tablespoon Italian seasoning
- 2 cups shredded mozzarella cheese

DIRECTIONS

1. Preheat oven to 350 degrees F (175 degrees C). Place the chicken breast halves on a baking sheet; bake 20 to 30 minutes, until no longer pink and juices run clear. Remove from heat, and set aside.
2. Increase the oven temperature to 400 degrees F (200 degrees C).
3. Melt the butter in a medium saucepan over medium heat. Stirring constantly, mix in the garlic, lemon juice, cream of mushroom soup, Italian seasoning, half-and-half, and Parmesan cheese.
4. Arrange the spinach over the bottom of a 9x9 inch baking dish. Cover the spinach with the mushrooms. Pour half the mixture from the saucepan over the mushrooms. Arrange chicken breasts in the dish, and cover with the remaining sauce mixture. Sprinkle with bacon bits, and top with mozzarella cheese.
5. Bake 20 to 25 minutes in the 400 degrees F (200 degrees C) oven, until bubbly and lightly browned.

SALSA CHICKEN RICE CASSEROLE
Servings: 8 | Prep: 20m | Cooks: 1h | Total: 1h20m

NUTRITION FACTS

Calories: 477 | Carbohydrates: 34.8g | Fat: 23.9g | Protein: 30g | Cholesterol: 88mg

INGREDIENTS

- 1 1/3 cups uncooked white rice
- 1 (10.75 ounce) can condensed cream of chicken soup
- 2 2/3 cups water
- 1 (10.75 ounce) can condensed cream of mushroom soup
- 4 skinless, boneless chicken breast halves
- 1 onion, chopped
- 2 cups shredded Monterey Jack cheese
- 1 1/2 cups mild salsa
- 2 cups shredded Cheddar cheese

DIRECTIONS

1. Place rice and water in a saucepan, and bring to a boil. Reduce heat to low, cover, and simmer for 20 minutes.
2. Meanwhile, place chicken breast halves into a large saucepan, and fill the pan with water. Bring to a boil, and cook for 20 minutes, or until done. Remove chicken from water. When cool enough to handle, cut meat into bite-size pieces.
3. Preheat oven to 350 degrees F (175 degrees C). Lightly grease a 9x13 inch baking dish.
4. In a medium bowl, combine Monterey Jack and Cheddar cheeses. In a separate bowl, mix together cream of chicken soup, cream of mushroom soup, onion, and salsa. Layer 1/2 of the rice, 1/2 of the chicken, 1/2 of the soup and salsa mixture, and 1/2 of the cheese mixture in prepared dish. Repeat layers, ending with cheese
5. Bake in preheated oven for about 40 minutes, or until bubbly.

CHEF JOHN'S MACARONI AND CHEESE

Servings: 6 | Prep: 15m | Cooks: 45m | Total: 1h

NUTRITION FACTS

Calories: 695 | Carbohydrates: 72.8g | Fat: 32.3g | Protein: 29.4g | Cholesterol: 95mg

INGREDIENTS

- 1 (16 ounce) package elbow macaroni
- 1 pinch ground nutmeg
- 1/4 cup butter
- 1/4 teaspoon Worcestershire sauce
- 1/4 cup all-purpose flour
- 1 teaspoon salt
- 1/4 teaspoon dried thyme
- 3 cups shredded sharp Cheddar cheese, divided
- 1/4 teaspoon cayenne pepper
- 1 teaspoon Dijon mustard
- 1/8 teaspoon white pepper
- 1/2 cup panko bread crumbs
- 3 cups milk
- 1 tablespoon butter, melted

DIRECTIONS

1. Preheat oven to 400 degrees F (200 degrees C).
2. Fill a large pot with lightly salted water and bring to a rolling boil over high heat. Once the water is boiling, stir in the macaroni, and return to a boil. Cook the pasta uncovered, stirring occasionally, until the pasta is cooked through but still slightly firm, about 8 minutes. Drain well.

3. Melt 1/4 cup butter in a large saucepan over medium heat. When the butter starts to foam and bubble, stir in the flour; cook on medium heat until flour just begins to turn pale yellow, 3 to 4 minutes. Add thyme, cayenne pepper, and white pepper; cook and stir another minute, then whisk in 1 cup of milk until smooth. Pour in remaining milk and whisk again. Bring the sauce just to a simmer.

4. Stir in nutmeg, Worcestershire sauce, and salt; simmer on medium-low heat until thickened, about 8 minutes, whisking often. Turn heat off, then add 2 1/4 cups of Cheddar cheese; stir until melted and combined. Add Dijon mustard.

5. Transfer the macaroni into a casserole dish, then pour in the cheese sauce; stir to thoroughly combine sauce with pasta. Mix panko bread crumbs and 1 tablespoon melted butter in a small bowl, and sprinkle crumbs on top of macaroni and cheese. Sprinkle remaining 3/4 cup of Cheddar cheese on top.

6. Bake in the preheated oven until bread crumbs and Cheddar cheese topping are golden brown, about 20 minutes.

SPANISH RICE BAKE

Servings: 6 | Prep: 15m | Cooks: 45m | Total: 1h

NUTRITION FACTS

Calories: 350 | Carbohydrates: 24.9g | Fat: 19.1g | Protein: 18.5g | Cholesterol: 67mg

INGREDIENTS

- 1 pound lean ground beef
- 1 teaspoon salt
- 1/2 cup finely chopped onion
- 1 teaspoon brown sugar
- 1/4 cup chopped green bell pepper
- 1/2 teaspoon ground cumin
- 1 (14.5 ounce) can canned tomatoes
- 1/2 teaspoon Worcestershire sauce
- 1 cup water
- 1 pinch ground black pepper
- 3/4 cup uncooked long grain rice
- 1/2 cup shredded Cheddar cheese
- 1/2 cup chile sauce
- 2 tablespoons chopped fresh cilantro

DIRECTIONS

1. Preheat oven to 375 degrees F (190 degrees C).

2. Brown the ground beef in a large skillet over medium-high heat. Drain excess fat and transfer beef to a large pot over medium low heat.. Stir in the onion, green bell pepper, tomatoes, water, rice, chile sauce, salt, brown sugar, cumin, Worcestershire sauce and ground black pepper.
3. Let this simmer for about 30 minutes, stirring occasionally, then transport this to a 2-quart casserole dish. Press down firmly and sprinkle with the shredded Cheddar cheese.
4. Bake at 375 degrees F (190 degrees C) for 10 to 15 minutes, or until cheese is melted and bubbly. Garnish with chopped fresh cilantro.

CHICKEN ENCHILADAS

Servings: 8 | Prep: 20m | Cooks: 25m | Total: 45m

NUTRITION FACTS

Calories: 352 | Carbohydrates: 30.6g | Fat: 16.9g | Protein: 19.2g | Cholesterol: 50mg

INGREDIENTS

- 1 (10.75 ounce) can condensed cream of chicken soup
- 2 cups chopped cooked chicken breast
- 1/2 cup sour cream
- 1 (4 ounce) can chopped green chile peppers, drained
- 1 tablespoon margarine
- 8 (8 inch) flour tortillas
- 1 onion, chopped
- 1 cup shredded Cheddar cheese
- 1 teaspoon chili powder

DIRECTIONS

1. Preheat oven to 350 degrees F (175 degrees C).
2. In a small bowl mix the soup and sour cream; set aside.
3. Melt margarine in a medium saucepan over medium high heat. Add onion and chili powder, and saute until tender. Stir in the chicken, chile peppers, and 2 tablespoons of the soup mixture. Cook and stir until heated through.
4. Spread 1/2 cup of the soup mixture in a 9x13 inch baking dish. Spoon about 1/4 cup of the chicken mixture down the center of each tortilla. Roll up tortillas, and place, seam-side-down, in the baking dish. Spoon remaining soup mixture on top, and sprinkle with cheese.
5. Bake 25 minutes in the preheated oven, or until bubbly and lightly browned.

SPINACH ENCHILADAS

Servings: 5 | Prep: 20m | Cooks: 20m | Total: 40m

NUTRITION FACTS

Calories: 510 | Carbohydrates: 32.3g | Fat: 36g | Protein: 18.2g | Cholesterol: 95mg

INGREDIENTS

- 1 tablespoon butter
- 1/2 cup sour cream
- 1/2 cup sliced green onions
- 2 cups shredded Monterey Jack cheese
- 2 cloves garlic, minced
- 10 (6 inch) corn tortillas
- 1 (10 ounce) package frozen chopped spinach , thawed, drained and squeezed dry
- 1 (19 ounce) can enchilada sauce
- 1 cup ricotta cheese

DIRECTIONS

1. Preheat the oven to 375 degrees F (190 degrees C).
2. Melt butter in a saucepan over medium heat. Add garlic and onion; cook for a few minutes until fragrant, but not brown. Stir in spinach, and cook for about 5 more minutes. Remove from the heat, and mix in ricotta cheese, sour cream, and 1 cup of Monterey Jack cheese.
3. In a skillet over medium heat, warm tortillas one at a time until flexible, about 15 seconds. Spoon about 1/4 cup of the spinach mixture onto the center of each tortilla. Roll up, and place seam side down in a 9x13 inch baking dish. Pour enchilada sauce over the top, and sprinkle with the remaining cup of Monterey Jack.
4. Bake for 15 to 20 minutes in the preheated oven, until sauce is bubbling and cheese is lightly browned at the edges.

CHEESY HAM AND HASH BROWN CASSEROLE
Servings: 12 | Prep: 15m | Cooks: 1h | Total: 1h15m

NUTRITION FACTS

Calories: 415 | Carbohydrates: 29.7g | Fat: 27.2g | Protein: 14.4g | Cholesterol: 53mg

INGREDIENTS

- 1 (32 ounce) package frozen hash brown potatoes
- 1 (16 ounce) container sour cream
- 8 ounces cooked, diced ham
- 2 cups shredded sharp Cheddar cheese
- 2 (10.75 ounce) cans condensed cream of potato soup
- 1 1/2 cups grated Parmesan cheese

DIRECTIONS

1. Preheat oven to 375 degrees F (190 degrees C). Lightly grease a 9x13 inch baking dish.
2. In a large bowl, mix hash browns, ham, cream of potato soup, sour cream, and Cheddar cheese. Spread evenly into prepared dish. Sprinkle with Parmesan cheese
3. Bake 1 hour in the preheated oven, or until bubbly and lightly brown. Serve immediately.

BEST TUNA CASSEROLE
Servings: 6 | Prep: 15m | Cooks: 20m | Total: 35m

NUTRITION FACTS

Calories: 595 | Carbohydrates: 58.1g | Fat: 26.1g | Protein: 32.1g | Cholesterol: 99mg

INGREDIENTS

- 1 (12 ounce) package egg noodles
- 2 (5 ounce) cans tuna, drained
- 1/4 cup chopped onion
- 2 (10.75 ounce) cans condensed cream of mushroom soup
- 2 cups shredded Cheddar cheese
- 1/2 (4.5 ounce) can sliced mushrooms
- 1 cup frozen green peas
- 1 cup crushed potato chips

DIRECTIONS

1. Bring a large pot of lightly salted water to a boil. Cook pasta in boiling water for 8 to 10 minutes, or until al dente; drain
2. Preheat oven to 425 degrees F (220 degrees C).
3. In a large bowl, thoroughly mix noodles, onion, 1 cup cheese, peas, tuna, soup and mushrooms. Transfer to a 9x13 inch baking dish, and top with potato chip crumbs and remaining 1 cup cheese.
4. Bake for 15 to 20 minutes in the preheated oven, or until cheese is bubbly.

EASY MEXICAN CASSEROLE
Servings: 6 | Prep: 20m | Cooks: 30m | Total: 50m

NUTRITION FACTS

Calories: 632 | Carbohydrates: 32.8g | Fat: 43.7g | Protein: 31.7g | Cholesterol: 119mg

INGREDIENTS

- 1 pound lean ground beef
- 1 (2 ounce) can sliced black olives, drained
- 2 cups salsa

- 1/2 cup chopped green onion
- 1 (16 ounce) can chili beans, drained
- 1/2 cup chopped fresh tomato
- 3 cups tortilla chips, crushed
- 2 cups shredded Cheddar cheese
- 2 cups sour cream

DIRECTIONS

1. Preheat oven to 350 degrees F (175 degrees C).
2. In a large skillet over medium-high heat, cook ground beef until no longer pink. Stir in salsa, reduce heat, and simmer 20 minutes, or until liquid is absorbed. Stir in beans, and heat through.
3. Spray a 9x13 baking dish with cooking spray. Spread crushed tortilla chips in dish, and then spoon beef mixture over chips. Spread sour cream over beef, and sprinkle olives, green onion, and tomato over the sour cream. Top with Cheddar cheese.
4. Bake in preheated oven for 30 minutes, or until hot and bubbly.

CHICKEN NOODLE CASSEROLE

Servings: 6 | Prep: 30m | Cooks: 30m | Total: 1h

NUTRITION FACTS

Calories: 542 | Carbohydrates: g | Fat: 34.2g | Protein: 23.3g | Cholesterol: 133mg

INGREDIENTS

- 4 skinless, boneless chicken breast halves
- salt to taste
- 6 ounces egg noodles
- ground black pepper to taste
- 1 (10.75 ounce) can condensed cream of mushroom soup
- 1 cup crumbled buttery round crackers
- 1 (10.75 ounce) can condensed cream of chicken soup
- 1/2 cup butter
- 1 cup sour cream

DIRECTIONS

1. Poach chicken in a large pot of simmering water. Cook until no longer pink in center, about 12 minutes. Remove from pot and set aside. Bring chicken cooking water to a boil and cook pasta in it. Drain. Cut chicken into small pieces, and mix with noodles.
2. In a separate bowl, mix together mushroom soup, chicken soup, and sour cream. Season with salt and pepper. Gently stir together cream soup mixture with the chicken mixture. Place in a 2 quart baking dish.

3. Melt butter in a small saucepan, and remove from heat. Stir in crumbled crackers. Top casserole with the buttery crackers.
4. Bake at 350 degrees F (175 degrees C) for about 30 minutes, until heated through and browned on top.

PIZZA CASSEROLE

Servings: 7 | Prep: 30m | Cooks: 30m | Total: 1h

NUTRITION FACTS

Calories: 386 | Carbohydrates: 17.7g | Fat: 25.3g | Protein: 20.2g | Cholesterol: 79mg

INGREDIENTS

- 2 cups uncooked egg noodles
- 1 cup sliced pepperoni sausage
- 1/2 pound lean ground beef
- 16 ounces pizza sauce
- 1 onion, chopped
- 4 tablespoons milk
- 2 cloves garlic, minced
- 1 cup shredded mozzarella cheese
- 1 green bell pepper, chopped

DIRECTIONS

1. Cook noodles according to package directions.
2. Preheat oven to 350 degrees F (175 degrees C).
3. In a medium skillet over medium-high heat, brown the ground beef with the onion, garlic and green bell pepper. Drain excess fat. Stir in the noodles, pepperoni, pizza sauce and milk, and mix well. Pour this mixture into a 2-quart casserole dish.
4. Bake at 350 degrees F (175 degrees C) for 20 minutes, top with the cheese, then bake for 5 to 10 more minutes.

TACO PIE

Servings: 8 | Prep: 20m | Cooks: 10m | Total: 30m

NUTRITION FACTS

Calories: 687 | Carbohydrates: 50.6g | Fat: 43.4g | Protein: 24.4g | Cholesterol: 100mg

INGREDIENTS

- 1 (8 ounce) package refrigerated crescent rolls

- 1 (16 ounce) container sour cream
- 1 pound ground beef
- 8 ounces shredded Mexican-style cheese blend
- 1 (1 ounce) package taco seasoning mix
- 1 (14 ounce) bag tortilla chips, crushed

DIRECTIONS

1. Preheat oven to 350 degrees F (175 degrees C).
2. Lay crescent dough flat on the bottom of a square cake pan and bake according to package directions.
3. Meanwhile, brown the ground beef in a large skillet over medium high heat. Add the taco seasoning and stir together well. When dough is done, remove from oven and place meat mixture on top, then layer with sour cream and cheese, and then top off with the crushed nacho chips.
4. Return to oven and bake at 350 degrees F (175 degrees C) for 10 minutes, or until cheese has melted.

BROCCOLI CHICKEN DIVAN

Servings: 6 | Prep: 20m | Cooks: 20m | Total: 40m

NUTRITION FACTS

Calories: 186 | Carbohydrates: 12.2g | Fat: 8.5g | Protein: 15.5g | Cholesterol: 44mg

INGREDIENTS

- 1 pound chopped fresh broccoli
- 1/2 cup shredded Cheddar cheese
- 1 ½ cups cubed, cooked chicken meat
- 1 tablespoon butter, melted
- 1 (10.75 ounce) can condensed cream of broccoli soup
- 2 tablespoons dried bread crumbs
- 1/3 cup milk

DIRECTIONS

1. Preheat oven to 450 degrees F (230 degrees C).
2. Place the broccoli in a saucepan with enough water to cover. Bring to a boil, and cook 5 minutes, or until tender. Drain.
3. Place the cooked broccoli in a 9 inch pie plate. Top with the chicken. In a bowl, mix the soup and milk, and pour over the chicken. Sprinkle with Cheddar cheese. Mix the melted butter with the bread crumbs, and sprinkle over the cheese.
4. Bake in the preheated oven for 15 minutes, or until bubbly and lightly brown.

CABBAGE ROLL CASSEROLE

Servings: 12 | Prep: 10m | Cooks: 1h30m | Total: 1h40m

NUTRITION FACTS

Calories: 352 | Carbohydrates: 25.5g | Fat: 20.6g | Protein: 17.1g | Cholesterol: 64mg

INGREDIENTS

- 2 pounds ground beef
- 1 cup uncooked white rice
- 1 cup chopped onion
- 1 teaspoon salt
- 1 (29 ounce) can tomato sauce
- 2 (14 ounce) cans beef broth
- 3 ½ pounds chopped cabbage

DIRECTIONS

1. Preheat oven to 350 degrees F (175 degrees C).
2. In a large skillet, brown beef in oil over medium high heat until redness is gone. Drain off fat.
3. In a large mixing bowl combine the onion, tomato sauce, cabbage, rice and salt. Add meat and mix all together. Pour mixture into a 9x13 inch baking dish. Pour broth over meat mixture and bake in the preheated oven, covered, for 1 hour. Stir, replace cover and bake for another 30 minutes.

TUNA NOODLE CASSEROLE FROM SCRATCH

Servings: 6 | Prep: 30m | Cooks: 45m | Total: 1h15m

NUTRITION FACTS

Calories: 546 | Carbohydrates: 39.9g | Fat: 31.2g | Protein: 27.2g | Cholesterol: 121mg

INGREDIENTS

- 1/2 cup butter, divided
- 2 cups milk
- 1 (8 ounce) package uncooked medium egg noodles
- salt and pepper to taste
- 1/2 medium onion, finely chopped
- 2 (5 ounce) cans tuna, drained and flaked
- 1 stalk celery, finely chopped
- 1 cup frozen peas, thawed
- 1 clove garlic, minced
- 3 tablespoons bread crumbs

- 8 ounces button mushrooms, sliced
- 2 tablespoons butter, melted
- 1/4 cup all-purpose flour
- 1 cup shredded Cheddar cheese

DIRECTIONS

1. Preheat oven to 375 degrees F (190 degrees C). Butter a medium baking dish with 1 tablespoon butter.
2. Bring a large pot of lightly salted water to a boil. Add egg noodles, cook for 8 to 10 minutes, until al dente, and drain.
3. Melt 1 tablespoon butter in a skillet over medium-low heat. Stir in the onion, celery, and garlic, and cook 5 minutes, until tender. Increase heat to medium-high, and mix in mushrooms. Continue to cook and stir 5 minutes, or until most of the liquid has evaporated.
4. Melt 4 tablespoons butter in a medium saucepan, and whisk in flour until smooth. Gradually whisk in milk, and continue cooking 5 minutes, until sauce is smooth and slightly thickened. Season with salt and pepper. Stir in tuna, peas, mushroom mixture, and cooked noodles. Transfer to the baking dish. Melt remaining 2 tablespoons butter in a small bowl, mix with bread crumbs, and sprinkle over the casserole. Top with cheese.
5. Bake 25 minutes in the preheated oven, or until bubbly and lightly browned.

UNSTUFFED CABBAGE ROLL

Servings: 6 | Prep: 20m | Cooks: 35m | Total: 55m

NUTRITION FACTS

Calories: 398 | Carbohydrates: 16.3g | Fat: 23.8g | Protein: 28.5g | Cholesterol: 93mg

INGREDIENTS

- 2 pounds ground beef
- 1/2 cup water
- 1 large onion, chopped
- 2 cloves garlic, minced
- 1 small head cabbage, chopped
- 2 teaspoons salt
- 2 (14.5 ounce) cans diced tomatoes
- 1 teaspoon ground black pepper
- 1 (8 ounce) can tomato sauce

DIRECTIONS

1. Heat a Dutch oven or large skillet over medium-high heat. Cook and stir beef and onion in the hot Dutch oven until browned and crumbly, 5 to 7 minutes; drain and discard grease. Add cabbage, tomatoes, tomato sauce, water, garlic, salt, and pepper and bring to a boil. Cover Dutch oven, reduce heat, and simmer until cabbage is tender, about 30 minutes.

SWISS CHICKEN CASSEROLE

Servings: 6 | Prep: 10m | Cooks: 50m | Total: 1h

NUTRITION FACTS

Calories: 430 | Carbohydrates: 19g | Fat: 20.8g | Protein: 38.5g | Cholesterol: 120mg

INGREDIENTS

- 6 skinless, boneless chicken breasts
- 1/4 cup milk
- 6 slices Swiss cheese
- 2 cups herb-seasoned stuffing mix
- 1 (10.75 ounce) can condensed cream of chicken soup
- 1/4 cup butter

DIRECTIONS

1. Preheat oven to 350 degrees F (175 degrees C).
2. Arrange chicken in a greased 12 x 8 x 2 baking dish. Top with Swiss cheese slices
3. Combine soup and milk and stir well. Spoon mixture over chicken and sprinkle with stuffing mix. Drizzle butter or margarine over crumbs.
4. Cover and bake at 350 degrees F (175 degrees C) for 50 minutes. Enjoy.

BAKED SPAGHETTI

Servings: 8 | Prep: 25m | Cooks: 1h | Total: 1h25m

NUTRITION FACTS

Calories: 728 | Carbohydrates: 61.9g | Fat: 33.6g | Protein: 42.5g | Cholesterol: 150mg

INGREDIENTS

- 1 (16 ounce) package spaghetti
- 2 eggs
- 1 pound ground beef
- 1/3 cup grated Parmesan cheese
- 1 onion, chopped
- 5 tablespoons butter, melted

- 1 (32 ounce) jar meatless spaghetti sauce
- 2 cups small curd cottage cheese, divided
- 1/2 teaspoon seasoned salt
- 4 cups shredded mozzarella cheese, divided

DIRECTIONS

1. Preheat oven to 350 degrees F (175 degrees C). Lightly grease a 9x13-inch baking dish.
2. Bring a large pot of lightly salted water to a boil. Cook spaghetti in boiling water, stirring occasionally until cooked through but firm to the bite, about 12 minutes. Drain.
3. Heat a large skillet over medium heat; cook and stir beef and onion until meat is browned and onions are soft and translucent, about 7 minutes. Drain. Stir in spaghetti sauce and seasoned salt.
4. Whisk eggs, Parmesan cheese, and butter in a large bowl. Mix in spaghetti to egg mixture and toss to coat. Place half the spaghetti mixture into baking dish. Top with half the cottage cheese, mozzarella, and meat sauce. Repeat layers. Cover with aluminum foil.
5. Bake in preheated oven for 40 minutes. Remove foil and continue to bake until the cheese is melted and lightly browned, 20 to 25 minutes longer.

EASY CHICKEN ENCHILADAS

Servings: 6 | Prep: 20m | Cooks: 30m | Total: 50m

NUTRITION FACTS

Calories: 565 | Carbohydrates: 32.8g | Fat: 34.1g | Protein: 32.6g | Cholesterol: 120mg

INGREDIENTS

- 1 (8 ounce) package cream cheese
- 1 (15.5 ounce) can pinto beans, drained
- 1 cup salsa
- 6 (6 inch) flour tortillas
- 2 cups chopped cooked chicken breast meat
- 2 cups shredded Colby-Jack cheese

DIRECTIONS

1. Preheat the oven to 350 degrees F (175 degrees C). Lightly grease a 9x13 inch baking dish.
2. In a small saucepan over medium heat, combine the cream cheese and salsa. Cook, stirring until melted and well blended. Stir in chicken and pinto beans. Fill tortillas with the mixture, roll and place into the prepared baking dish. Spread cheese over the top. Cover with aluminum foil.
3. Bake for 30 minutes, or until heated through. Garnish with your favorite toppings such as lettuce and tomatoes, or sour cream

SAUSAGE CASSEROLE

Servings: 12 | Prep: 25m | Cooks: 1h15m | Total: 1h45m | Additional: 5m

NUTRITION FACTS

Calories: 355 | Carbohydrates: 7.9g | Fat: 26.3g | Protein: 21.6g | Cholesterol: 188mg

INGREDIENTS

- 1 pound sage flavored breakfast sausage
- 1/2 cup onion, shredded
- 3 cups shredded potatoes, drained and pressed
- 1 (16 ounce) container small curd cottage cheese
- 1/4 cup butter, melted
- 6 jumbo eggs
- 12 ounces mild Cheddar cheese, shredded

DIRECTIONS

1. Preheat oven to 375 degrees F (190 degrees C). Lightly grease a 9x13 inch square baking dish.
2. Place sausage in a large, deep skillet. Cook over medium-high heat until evenly brown. Drain, crumble, and set aside.
3. In the prepared baking dish, stir together the shredded potatoes and butter. Line the bottom and sides of the baking dish with the mixture. In a bowl, mix the sausage, Cheddar cheese, onion, cottage cheese, and eggs. Pour over the potato mixture.
4. Bake 1 hour in the preheated oven, or until a toothpick inserted into center of the casserole comes out clean. Let cool for 5 minutes before serving.

HAMBURGER POTATO CASSEROLE

Servings: 6 | Prep: 20m | Cooks: 1h | Total: 1h30m

NUTRITION FACTS

Calories: 26.9 | Carbohydrates: 17.1g | Fat: 26.9g | Protein: 22.1g | Cholesterol: 83mg

INGREDIENTS

- 1 pound lean ground beef
- 3/4 cup milk
- 3 cups peeled and thinly sliced potatoes
- salt to taste
- 1 (10.75 ounce) can condensed cream of mushroom soup
- freshly ground pepper, to taste
- 1/2 cup chopped onion

- 1 cup shredded Cheddar cheese

DIRECTIONS

1. Preheat oven to 350 degrees F (175 degrees C).
2. In a medium skillet over medium heat, brown the ground beef; drain fat.
3. In a medium mixing bowl, combine cream of mushroom soup, onion, milk, salt and pepper to taste.
4. Alternately layer the potatoes, soup mixture and meat in a 11x7 inch (2 quart) baking dish. Bake in the preheated oven for 1 to 1 1/2 hours, or until potatoes are tender. Top with Cheddar cheese, and continue baking until cheese is melted.

CHILI RELLENOS CASSEROLE

Servings: 6 | Prep: 15m | Cooks: 45m | Total: 1h

NUTRITION FACTS

Calories: 387 | Carbohydrates: 12g | Fat: 27.6g | Protein: 23.9g | Cholesterol: 140mg

INGREDIENTS

- 2 (7 ounce) cans whole green chile peppers, drained
- 1 (5 ounce) can evaporated milk
- 8 ounces Monterey Jack cheese, shredded
- 2 tablespoons all-purpose flour
- 8 ounces Longhorn or Cheddar cheese, shredded
- 1/2 cup milk
- 2 eggs, beaten
- 1 (8 ounce) can tomato sauce

DIRECTIONS

1. Preheat oven to 350 degrees F (175 degrees C). Spray a 9x13-inch baking dish with cooking spray.
2. Lay half of the chilies evenly in bottom of baking dish. Sprinkle with half of the Jack and Cheddar cheeses, and cover with remaining chilies. In a bowl, mix together the eggs, milk, and flour, and pour over the top of the chilies.
3. Bake in the preheated oven for 25 minutes. Remove from oven, pour tomato sauce evenly over the top, and continue baking another 15 minutes. Sprinkle with remaining Jack and Cheddar cheeses, and serve.

MEXICAN CASSEROLE

Servings: 5 | Prep: 15m | Cooks: 15m | Total: 30m

NUTRITION FACTS

Calories: 384 | Carbohydrates: 34g | Fat: 16.6g | Protein: 26.8g | Cholesterol: 59mg

INGREDIENTS

- 2 tablespoons vegetable oil
- 1/4 cup salsa
- 3/4 pound cubed skinless, boneless chicken breast meat
- water as needed
- 1/2 (1.25 ounce) package taco seasoning mix
- 1 cup shredded Mexican-style cheese
- 1 (15 ounce) can black beans, rinsed and drained
- 1 1/2 cups crushed plain tortilla chips
- 1 (8.75 ounce) can sweet corn, drained

DIRECTIONS

1. In a large skillet over medium high heat, saute chicken in oil until cooked through and no longer pink inside. Add taco seasoning, beans, corn, salsa and a little water to prevent drying out. Cover skillet and simmer over medium low heat for 10 minutes.
2. Preheat oven to 350 degrees F (175 degrees C).
3. Transfer chicken mixture to a 9x13 inch baking dish. Top with 1/2 cup of the cheese and crushed tortilla chips.
4. Bake in the preheated oven for 15 minutes. Add remaining 1/2 cup cheese and bake until cheese is melted and bubbly.

SPINACH AND FETA PITA BAKE

Servings: 6 | Prep: 10m | Cooks: 12m | Total: 22m

NUTRITION FACTS

Calories: 350 | Carbohydrates: 41.6g | Fat: 17.1g | Protein: 11.6g | Cholesterol: 13mg

INGREDIENTS

- 1 (6 ounce) tub sun-dried tomato pesto
- 1/2 cup crumbled feta cheese
- 6 (6 inch) whole wheat pita breads
- 2 tablespoons grated Parmesan cheese
- 2 roma (plum) tomatoes, chopped
- 3 tablespoons olive oil
- 1 bunch spinach, rinsed and chopped
- ground black pepper to taste
- 4 fresh mushrooms, sliced

DIRECTIONS

1. Preheat the oven to 350 degrees F (175 degrees C).
2. Spread tomato pesto onto one side of each pita bread and place them pesto-side up on a baking sheet. Top pitas with tomatoes, spinach, mushrooms, feta cheese, and Parmesan cheese; drizzle with olive oil and season with pepper.
3. Bake in the preheated oven until pita breads are crisp, about 12 minutes. Cut pitas into quarters.

TACO CASSEROLE
Servings: 10 | Prep: 25m | Cooks: 35m | Total: 1h

NUTRITION FACTS

Calories: 334 | Carbohydrates: 28.2g | Fat: 17g | Protein: 15.6g | Cholesterol: 50mg

INGREDIENTS

- 1 pound lean ground beef
- 2 ounces shredded Cheddar cheese
- 8 ounces macaroni
- 2 ounces shredded Monterey Jack cheese
- 1/2 cup chopped onion
- 1 cup crushed tortilla chips
- 1 (10.75 ounce) can condensed tomato soup
- 1/2 cup sour cream (optional)
- 1 (14.5 ounce) can diced tomatoes
- 1/4 cup chopped green onions
- 1 (1.25 ounce) package taco seasoning mix

DIRECTIONS

1. Preheat oven to 350 degrees F (175 degrees C).
2. Cook pasta in a large pot of boiling water until al dente. Drain.
3. In a large skillet, cook and stir ground beef and chopped onion over medium heat until brown. Mix in tomato soup, diced tomatoes, and taco seasoning mix. Stir in pasta.
4. Spoon beef mixture into a 9x13 inch baking dish. Sprinkle crumbled taco chips and grated cheese on top.
5. Bake for 30 to 35 minutes, until the cheese is melted. Serve with chopped green onions and sour cream, if desired.

GROUND BEEF ENCHILADAS
Servings: 6 | Prep: 15m | Cooks: 40m | Total: 55m

NUTRITION FACTS

Calories: 556 | Carbohydrates: 26.1g | Fat: 33.8g | Protein: 34.8g | Cholesterol: 116mg

INGREDIENTS

- 1 1/2 pounds lean ground beef
- 1 cup plain yogurt
- 1 bunch green onions, finely chopped
- 1 (10.75 ounce) can condensed cream of chicken soup
- 1 diced fresh jalapeno pepper, or to taste
- 2 cups shredded mozzarella cheese
- 1/4 cup water
- 6 (6 inch) corn tortillas
- 1 (1.25 ounce) package taco seasoning mix

DIRECTIONS

1. Preheat oven to 350 degrees F (175 degrees C).
2. In a large skillet over medium heat, cook the ground beef, green onion, and jalapeno pepper until the beef is evenly brown. Stir in water and taco seasoning. Simmer until water has evaporated.
3. In a medium bowl, mix together yogurt, condensed soup, and cheese.
4. Divide the meat mixture evenly between tortillas. Place a couple of tablespoons of cheese mixture over meat, and roll up. Place in a 7x11 inch baking dish. Repeat for each tortilla. Spoon remaining cheese mixture over the top of the tortillas.
5. Bake in preheated oven for 20 to 30 minutes.

TURKEY TETRAZZINI

Servings: 8 | Prep: 20m | Cooks: 1h | Total: 1h20m

NUTRITION FACTS

Calories: 565 | Carbohydrates: 51.7g | Fat: 22.1g | Protein: 37.6g | Cholesterol: 105mg

INGREDIENTS

- 1 (16 ounce) package uncooked spaghetti
- 2 cups milk
- 1/2 cup butter
- 1 2/3 cups grated Parmesan cheese
- 1/2 cup all-purpose flour
- 4 cups chopped cooked turkey
- 3 cups chicken broth

DIRECTIONS

1. Preheat oven to 350 degrees F (175 degrees C). Lightly grease a baking dish.
2. Bring a large pot of lightly salted water to a boil. Add spaghetti, and cook for 8 to 10 minutes or until al dente. Drain, and place in the prepared baking dish.
3. Melt butter in a medium saucepan over medium heat. Stir in flour. Mix in chicken broth and milk. Cook and stir until the mixture comes to a boil. Stir in about 1 1/3 cups Parmesan cheese, and remove from heat.
4. Mix chicken broth mixture and turkey with spaghetti. Top with remaining cheese. Bake 1 hour in the preheated oven, until surface is lightly browned.

QUICK AND EASY GREEN CHILE CHICKEN ENCHILADA CASSEROLE

Servings: 8 | Prep: 30m | Cooks: 1h30m | Total: 2h

NUTRITION FACTS

Calories: 488 | Carbohydrates: 32.6g | Fat: 25.2g | Protein: 33.1g | Cholesterol: 95mg

INGREDIENTS

- 4 skinless, boneless chicken breast halves
- 1 (28 ounce) can green chile enchilada sauce
- garlic salt to taste
- 1 (16 ounce) package shredded Monterey Jack cheese
- 18 (6 inch) corn tortillas, torn in half
- 1 (8 ounce) container reduced fat sour cream

DIRECTIONS

1. Preheat oven to 350 degrees F (175 degrees C). Lightly grease a medium baking dish.
2. Season chicken with garlic salt. Arrange in the prepared baking dish. Bake 45 minutes in the preheated oven, until no longer pink and juices run clear. Cool, shred, and set aside.
3. With metal tongs, char each tortilla half over the open flame of a gas stove burner for about 1 minute, until lightly puffed.
4. Pour about 1/2 inch enchilada sauce in the bottom of a medium baking dish, and arrange 6 tortillas in a single layer. Top with 1/2 the chicken, 1/3 cheese, 1/2 the sour cream, and 1/3 of the remaining enchilada sauce. Repeat. Coat remaining tortillas thoroughly with remaining enchilada sauce, and arrange on top of the layers. Sprinkle with remaining cheese, and top with any remaining enchilada sauce
5. Cover, and bake 45 minutes in the preheated oven. Cool slightly before serving.

BROCCOLI, RICE, CHEESE, AND CHICKEN CASSEROLE

Servings: 8 | Prep: 15m | Cooks: 30m | Total: 45m

NUTRITION FACTS

Calories: 756 | Carbohydrates: 82.7g | Fat: 30.8g | Protein: 36g | Cholesterol: 110mg

INGREDIENTS

- 2 cups water
- 1/4 cup butter
- 2 cups uncooked instant rice
- 1 cup milk
- 2 (10 ounce) cans chunk chicken, drained
- 1 (16 ounce) package frozen chopped broccoli
- 1 (10.75 ounce) can condensed cream of mushroom soup
- 1 small white onion, chopped
- 1 (10.75 ounce) can condensed cream of chicken soup
- 1 pound processed cheese food

DIRECTIONS

1. Preheat oven to 350 degrees F (175 degrees C).
2. In a medium saucepan, bring the water to a boil. Mix in the instant rice, cover, and remove from heat. Let stand 5 minut
3. In a 9x13 inch baking dish, mix the prepared rice, chicken, cream of mushroom soup, cream of chicken soup, butter, milk, broccoli, onion, and processed cheese.
4. Bake in the preheated oven for 30 to 35 minutes, or until cheese is melted. Stir halfway through cooking to help cheese melt evenly.

BEEF NACHO CASSEROLE

Servings: 6 | Prep: 15m | Cooks: 20m | Total: 35m

NUTRITION FACTS

Calories: 497 | Carbohydrates: 23.9g | Fat: 33.6g | Protein: 26.1g | Cholesterol: 98mg

INGREDIENTS

- 1 pound ground beef
- 1 teaspoon chili powder
- 1 1/2 cups chunky salsa
- 2 cups crushed tortilla chips
- 1 (10 ounce) can whole kernel corn, drained

- 2 cups Colby cheese
- 3/4 cup creamy salad dressing (e.g. Miracle Whip)

DIRECTIONS

1. Preheat the oven to 350 degrees F (175 degrees C).
2. Place ground beef in a large skillet over medium-high heat. Cook, stirring to crumble, until evenly browned. Drain grease. Remove from the heat, and stir the salsa, corn, mayonnaise and chili powder into the beef. In a 2 quart casserole dish, layer the ground beef mixture, tortilla chips and cheese twice, ending with cheese on top
3. Bake for 20 minutes uncovered in the preheated oven, until cheese is melted and dish is thoroughly heated.

QUICK AND EASY MEXICAN CHICKEN
Servings: 4 | Prep: 15m | Cooks: 25m | Total: 40m

NUTRITION FACTS

Calories: 264 | Carbohydrates: 4.9g | Fat: 11.1g | Protein: 35.4g | Cholesterol: 98mg

INGREDIENTS

- 4 skinless, boneless chicken breasts
- 1 pinch ground black pepper
- cooking spray
- 1 pinch ground cumin
- 1 clove garlic, minced
- 1 cup salsa
- 1 pinch salt
- 1 cup shredded Cheddar cheese

DIRECTIONS

1. Preheat oven to 375 degrees F (190 degrees C).
2. Heat a greased skillet to medium. Rub chicken pieces with garlic, salt, pepper and cumin to taste; place in hot skillet. Cook until brown on both sides and no longer pink, 10 to 15 minutes.
3. Transfer chicken to 9x13-inch baking dish or casserole dish, top with salsa and cheese, and bake in preheated oven until cheese is bubbly and starts to brown, 15 to 20 minutes.

SEVEN LAYER TORTILLA PIE
Servings: 6 | Prep: 15m | Cooks: 40m | Total: 55m

NUTRITION FACTS

Calories: 405 | Carbohydrates: 54.8g | Fat: 11.7g | Protein: 21.1g | Cholesterol: 16mg

INGREDIENTS

- 2 (15 ounce) cans pinto beans, drained and rinsed
- 1/2 cup chopped tomatoes
- 1 cup salsa, divided
- 7 (8 inch) flour tortillas
- 2 cloves garlic, minced
- 2 cups shredded reduced-fat Cheddar cheese
- 2 tablespoons chopped fresh cilantro
- 1 cup salsa
- 1 (15 ounce) can black beans, rinsed and drained
- 1/2 cup sour cream

DIRECTIONS

1. Preheat oven to 400 degrees F (200 degrees C).
2. In a large bowl, mash pinto beans. Stir in 3/4 cup salsa and garlic.
3. In a separate bowl, mix together 1/4 cup salsa, cilantro, black beans and tomatoes.
4. Place 1 tortilla in a pie plate or tart dish. Spread 3/4 cup pinto bean mixture over tortilla to within 1/2 inch of edge. Top with 1/4 cup cheese, and cover with another tortilla. Spread with 2/3 cup black bean mixture, and top with 1/4 cup cheese. Repeat layering twice. Cover with remaining tortilla, and spread with remaining pinto bean mixture and cheese.
5. Cover with foil, and bake in preheated oven for about 40 minutes. Cut into wedges, and serve with salsa and sour cream.

PORTOBELLO PENNE PASTA CASSEROLE

Servings: 8 | Prep: 30m | Cooks: 30m | Total: 45m

NUTRITION FACTS

Calories: 380 | Carbohydrates: 32.1g | Fat: 21.3g | Protein: 16g | Cholesterol: 26mg

INGREDIENTS

- 1 (8 ounce) package uncooked penne pasta
- 1/2 teaspoon dried basil
- 2 tablespoons vegetable oil
- 2 cups milk
- 1/2 pound portobello mushrooms, thinly sliced
- 2 cups shredded mozzarella cheese
- 1/2 cup margarine
- 1 (10 ounce) package frozen chopped spinach, thawed

- 1/4 cup all-purpose flour
- 1/4 cup soy sauce
- 1 large clove garlic, minced

DIRECTIONS

1. Preheat oven to 350 degrees F (175 degrees C). Lightly grease a 9x13 inch baking dish.
2. Bring a large pot of lightly salted water to a boil. Place pasta in the pot, cook for 8 to 10 minutes, until al dente, and drain.
3. Heat the oil in a saucepan over medium heat. Stir in the mushrooms, cook 1 minute, and set aside. Melt margarine in the saucepan. Mix in flour, garlic, and basil. Gradually mix in milk until thickened. Stir in 1 cup cheese until melted. Remove saucepan from heat, and mix in cooked pasta, mushrooms, spinach, and soy sauce. Transfer to the prepared baking dish, and top with remaining cheese.
4. Bake 20 minutes in the preheated oven, until bubbly and lightly brown.

LAYERED CHICKEN AND BLACK BEAN ENCHILADA CASSEROLE

Servings: 8 | Prep: 25m | Cooks: 45m | Total: 1h10m

NUTRITION FACTS

Calories: 366 | Carbohydrates: 16.4g | Fat: 23.7g | Protein: 23g | Cholesterol: 92mg

INGREDIENTS

- 2 cups diced chicken breast meat
- 1 (4.5 ounce) can diced green chile peppers, drained
- 1/2 teaspoon ground cumin
- 1 (10 ounce) can red enchilada sauce
- 1/2 teaspoon ground coriander
- 8 (6 inch) corn tortillas
- 2 tablespoons chopped fresh cilantro
- 2 cups shredded Mexican blend cheese
- 1 (15 ounce) can black beans, rinsed and drained
- 1 (8 ounce) container sour cream

DIRECTIONS

1. Preheat the oven to 375 degrees F (190 degrees C).
2. Heat a large skillet over medium heat, and spray with vegetable cooking spray. Saute chicken with cumin and coriander until chicken is cooked through. Transfer to a medium bowl. Stir in the cilantro, black beans, and green chile peppers.

3. Spread half of the enchilada sauce over the bottom of an 11x7 inch baking dish. Place 4 tortillas over the sauce, overlapping if necessary. Spoon half of the chicken mixture over the tortillas, and sprinkle with half of the cheese and half of the sour cream. Spoon the remaining enchilada sauce over the cheese, and make another layer of tortillas. Layer the remaining chicken mixture over the tortillas. Cover dish with a lid or aluminum foil.
4. Bake for 30 minutes in the preheated oven. Remove the cover, and sprinkle the remaining cheese over the top and dot with sour cream. Continue cooking, uncovered, for an additional 5 to 10 minutes, or until cheese melts. Let stand 10 minutes before serving.

CHICKEN TETRAZZINI
Servings: 4 | Prep: 15m | Cooks: 45m | Total: 1h

NUTRITION FACTS

Calories: 730 | Carbohydrates: 52.7g | Fat: 42.6g | Protein: 33.1g | Cholesterol: 173mg

INGREDIENTS

- 1 (8 ounce) package spaghetti, broken into pieces
- 1 cup heavy cream
- 1/4 cup butter
- 2 tablespoons sherry
- 1/4 cup all-purpose flour
- 1 (4.5 ounce) can sliced mushrooms, drained
- 3/4 teaspoon salt
- 2 cups chopped cooked chicken
- 1/4 teaspoon ground black pepper
- 1/2 cup grated Parmesan cheese
- 1 cup chicken broth

DIRECTIONS

1. Preheat oven to 350 degrees F (175 degrees C). Lightly grease a 9x13 inch baking dish.
2. Bring a large pot of lightly salted water to a boil. Add spaghetti, and cook for 8 to 10 minutes, or until al dente; drain.
3. Meanwhile, in a large saucepan, melt butter over low heat. Stir in flour, salt, and pepper. Cook, stirring, until smooth. Remove from heat, and gradually stir in chicken broth and cream.
4. Return to heat, and bring to a low boil for 1 minute, stirring constantly. Add sherry, then stir in cooked spaghetti, mushrooms, and chicken. Pour mixture into the prepared baking dish, and top with Parmesan cheese.
5. Bake 30 minutes in the preheated oven, until bubbly and lightly browned.

MAMAW'S CHICKEN AND RICE CASSEROLE

Servings: 6 | Prep: 10m | Cooks: 1h | Total: 1h20m | Additional: 10m

NUTRITION FACTS

Calories: 441 | Carbohydrates: 36.7g | Fat: 25g | Protein: 16.8g | Cholesterol: 81mg

INGREDIENTS

- 3 chicken breasts, cut into cubes
- 1 (10.75 ounce) can cream of celery soup
- 2 cups water
- 1 (10.75 ounce) can cream of mushroom soup
- 2 cups instant white rice
- salt and ground black pepper to taste
- 1 (10.75 ounce) can cream of chicken soup
- 1/2 cup butter, sliced into pats

DIRECTIONS

1. Preheat oven to 400 degrees F (200 degrees C). Grease sides and bottom of a casserole dish.
2. Stir chicken, water, rice, cream of chicken soup, cream of celery soup, and cream of mushroom soup together in the prepared casserole dish; season with salt and pepper. Arrange butter evenly over the top of the chicken mixture.
3. Bake in preheated oven until the rice is tender and the chicken is cooked through, 1 hour to 75 minutes. Cool 15 minutes before serving.

TATER TOT TACO CASSEROLE

Servings: 8 | Prep: 15m | Cooks: 1h | Total: 1h15m

NUTRITION FACTS

Calories: 477 | Carbohydrates: 38.4g | Fat: 27g | Protein: 24.9g | Cholesterol: 76mg

INGREDIENTS

- 1 pound ground beef
- 1 (12 ounce) can black beans, rinsed and drained
- 1 small onion, diced
- 1 (12 ounce) bag shredded Mexican cheese blend
- 1 clove garlic, minced
- 1 (16 ounce) package frozen tater tots
- 1 (1 ounce) packet taco seasoning mix
- 1 (12 fluid ounce) can enchilada sauce

* 1 (16 ounce) bag frozen Mexican-style corn

DIRECTIONS

1. Preheat an oven to 375 degrees F (190 degrees C). Prepare a 9x13-inch baking dish with cooking spray.
2. Cook the ground beef in a skillet over medium heat until completely browned, 5 to 7 minutes. Add the onion, garlic, taco seasoning mix, frozen Mexican-style corn, and black beans to the ground beef; cook and stir another 10 minutes. Set aside to cool slightly.
3. Combine the ground beef mixture in a large bowl with about 3/4 of the Mexican cheese blend and the tater tots; stir to combine.
4. Pour about 1/3 of the enchilada sauce into the bottom of the prepared baking dish. Add the tater tot mixture to the baking dish; lightly pat the mixture down into a solid, even layer. Pour the remaining enchilada sauce over the tater tot layer.
5. Bake in the preheated oven for 40 minutes. Sprinkle the remaining Mexican cheese over the casserole and return to oven until the cheese is melted and bubbly, about 5 minutes more.

SKILLET PORK CHOPS WITH POTATOES AND ONION

Servings: 4 | Prep: 20m | Cooks: 50m | Total: 1h10m

NUTRITION FACTS

Calories: 354 | Carbohydrates: 31.2g | Fat: 16.4g | Protein: 20.9g | Cholesterol: 44mg

INGREDIENTS

* 2 tablespoons vegetable oil
* 4 Yukon Gold potatoes, thinly sliced
* 4 pork chops (1/2 inch thick), trimmed
* 2 medium onions, sliced
* 2 tablespoons all-purpose flour
* 3 cubes beef bouillon
* 1/3 cup grated Parmesan cheese
* 3/4 cup hot water
* 1/2 teaspoon salt
* 1 tablespoon lemon juice
* 1/4 teaspoon pepper

DIRECTIONS

1. Heat oil in a large skillet over medium heat. Coat the pork chops with flour, and place in the skillet. Brown about 4 minutes on each side.

2. In a small bowl, mix the Parmesan cheese, salt, and pepper. Sprinkle 1/2 the Parmesan cheese mixture over the pork chops. Layer chops with the potatoes. Sprinkle with remaining Parmesan cheese mixture. Top with onion slices.

3. In a small bowl, dissolve the beef bouillon cubes in hot water. Stir in the lemon juice. Pour over the layered pork chops.

4. Cover skillet, and reduce heat. Simmer 40 minutes, until vegetables are tender and pork chops have reached an internal temperature of 145 degrees F (63 degrees C).

CINDY'S JAMBALAYA

Servings: 8 | Prep: 20m | Cooks: 45m | Total: 1h10m | Additional: 5m

NUTRITION FACTS

Calories: 284 | Carbohydrates: 24.6g | Fat: 11.5g | Protein: 18.4g | Cholesterol: 107mg

INGREDIENTS

- 1 tablespoon olive oil
- 1 cup uncooked white rice
- 1/2 pound smoked sausage (such as Conecuh(C)), cut into 1/4-inch thick slices
- 1 (14.5 ounce) can diced tomatoes with juice
- 1 large onion, chopped
- 1 tablespoon minced garlic
- 1 cup chopped green bell pepper
- 2 cups chicken broth
- 1 cup chopped celery
- 3 bay leaves
- salt to taste
- 1/4 teaspoon dried thyme leaves
- 1/2 teaspoon Cajun seasoning, or to taste
- 1 pound peeled and deveined medium shrimp (30-40 per pound)

DIRECTIONS

1. Heat the olive oil in a Dutch oven or large pot over medium heat. Stir in the sausage, and cook for 2 minutes. Add the onion, bell pepper, and celery; season with salt and Cajun seasoning. Cook and stir until the vegetables are soft, 6 to 8 minutes. Stir in the rice until evenly coated in the vegetable mixture, then pour in the tomatoes with juice, garlic, chicken broth, bay leaves, and thyme leaves. Bring to a simmer over medium-high heat, then reduce heat to medium-low, cover, and simmer 20 minutes.

2. After 20 minutes, stir in the shrimp, and cook 10 minutes uncovered until the shrimp turn pink and are no longer translucent in the center. Remove the pot from the heat, and let stand 5 minutes. Discard the bay leaves before serving.

CHICKEN ENCHILADA CASSEROLE

Servings: 12 | Prep: 30m | Cooks: 30m | Total: 1h

NUTRITION FACTS

Calories: 537 | Carbohydrates: 39.9g | Fat: 28.1g | Protein: 31.4g | Cholesterol: 95mg

INGREDIENTS

- 1 (16 ounce) container sour cream
- 1 (8 ounce) can chili beans, drained
- 1 (16 ounce) jar salsa
- 6 (12 inch) flour tortillas, cut into strips
- 1 (10.75 ounce) can condensed cream of chicken soup
- 6 skinless, boneless chicken breast halves - cooked and shredded
- 1/4 cup diced onion
- 4 cups shredded Cheddar cheese

DIRECTIONS

1. Preheat oven to 350 degrees F (175 degrees C).
2. In a large bowl, mix sour cream, salsa, cream of chicken soup, onion and chili beans.
3. Layer the bottom of a 9x13 inch baking dish with 1/3 tortilla strips. Top with 1/3 chicken, 1/3 sour cream mixture and 1/3 Cheddar cheese. Repeat layering with remaining ingredients.
4. Bake in the preheated oven 20 to 30 minutes, or until golden and bubbly. Let stand about 10 minutes, or as long as you can stand it!!! You're done.

MANICOTTI ITALIAN CASSEROLE

Servings: 8 | Prep: 10m | Cooks: 30m | Total: 40m

NUTRITION FACTS

Calories: 909 | Carbohydrates: 77.6g | Fat: 43g | Protein: 52.1g | Cholesterol: 127mg

INGREDIENTS

- 1 pound rigatoni pasta
- 2 (32 ounce) jars spaghetti sauce
- 1 pound ground beef
- 1 1/2 pounds shredded mozzarella cheese
- 1 pound Italian sausage
- thinly sliced pepperoni
- 1 (8 ounce) can mushrooms, drained

DIRECTIONS

1. Preheat oven to 350 degrees F (175 degrees C).
2. Bring a large pot of lightly salted water to boil. Pour in rigatoni, and cook until al dente, about 8 to 10 minutes. Drain, and set pasta aside.
3. Meanwhile, brown ground beef and italian sausage in a large skillet over medium heat. With a slotted spoon, remove beef and sausage to a baking dish. Stir mushrooms, spaghetti sauce, and cooked pasta into the baking dish. Sprinkle cheese and pepperoni over the top.
4. Bake in preheated oven until the cheese is brown and bubbly, about 20 minutes.

PESTO CHICKEN PENNE CASSEROLE
Servings: 12 | Prep: 15m | Cooks: 1h | Total: 1h15m

NUTRITION FACTS

Calories: 760 | Carbohydrates: 40.7g | Fat: 47.2g | Protein: 45.4g | Cholesterol: 114mg

INGREDIENTS

- 1/2 cup seasoned bread crumbs
- 3 cups fresh baby spinach
- 1/2 cup grated Parmesan cheese
- 1 (15 ounce) can crushed tomatoes
- 1 tablespoon olive oil
- 1 (15 ounce) jar Alfredo sauce
- 1 (16 ounce) box penne pasta
- 1 (15 ounce) jar pesto sauce
- 6 cups cubed cooked chicken
- 1 1/2 cups milk
- 4 cups shredded Italian cheese blend

DIRECTIONS

1. Preheat an oven to 350 degrees F (175 degrees C). Grease a 9x13-inch baking dish. Combine the bread crumbs, Parmesan cheese, and olive oil in a small bowl until evenly moistened; set aside.
2. Fill a large pot with lightly salted water and bring to a rolling boil over high heat. Once the water is boiling, stir in the penne, and return to a boil. Cook the pasta uncovered, stirring occasionally, until the pasta has cooked through, but is still firm to the bite, about 11 minutes. Drain well in a colander set in the sink.
3. Meanwhile, combine the chicken in a bowl with the Italian cheese blend, spinach, tomatoes, alfredo sauce, pesto sauce, and milk. Stir in the pasta once done, and scoop into the prepared baking dish. Top with the bread crumb mixture.
4. Bake in the preheated oven until bubbly and golden brown on top, 40 to 45 minutes.

CHILI DOG CASSEROLE

Servings: 10 | Prep: 15m | Cooks: 30m | Total: 45m

NUTRITION FACTS

Calories: 491 | Carbohydrates: 39.4g | Fat: 28.8g | Protein: 19.7g | Cholesterol: 62mg

INGREDIENTS

- 2 (15 ounce) cans chili with beans
- 10 (8 inch) flour tortillas
- 1 (16 ounce) package beef frankfurters
- 1 (8 ounce) package Cheddar cheese, shredded

DIRECTIONS

1. Preheat oven to 425 degrees F (220 degrees C).
2. Spread 1 can of chili and beans in the bottom of a 9x13 inch baking dish. Roll up franks inside tortillas and place in baking dish, seam side down, on top of chili and bean 'bed'. Top with remaining can of chili and beans, and sprinkle with cheese.
3. Cover baking dish with aluminum foil, and bake at 425 degrees F (220 degrees C) for 30 minutes.

SERBIAN GROUND BEEF, VEGGIE, AND POTATO BAKE

Servings: 4 | Prep: 25m | Cooks: 1h | Total: 1h25m

NUTRITION FACTS

Calories: 367 | Carbohydrates: 27.2g | Fat: 18.1g | Protein: 22.7g | Cholesterol: 72mg

INGREDIENTS

- 1 pound ground beef
- 1/4 teaspoon crushed red pepper
- 1 tablespoon olive oil
- 1 pinch ground cinnamon
- 1 green bell pepper, chopped
- 1 pinch ground cloves
- 1 onion, chopped
- 1/4 cup water
- 1 carrot, shredded
- 1/8 cup red wine
- 2 celery stalks, chopped
- 1 cube beef bouillon
- 1/2 tablespoon paprika

- 2 tablespoons half-and-half
- 1/2 teaspoon salt
- 2 potatoes, peeled and sliced
- 3/4 teaspoon black pepper

DIRECTIONS

1. Preheat oven to 400 degrees F (200 degrees C). Lightly grease a casserole dish.
2. In a skillet over medium heat, cook the beef until evenly brown. Remove beef from skillet, reserving juices, and set aside. Mix in the olive oil, and saute the green pepper, onion, carrot, and celery until tender.
3. Return beef to the skillet, and season with paprika, salt, black pepper, red pepper, cinnamon, and cloves. Stir in the water and red wine until heated through. Dissolve the beef bouillon cube into the mixture. Remove skillet from heat, and mix in the half-and-half.
4. Layer the bottom of the prepared casserole dish with enough potato slices to cover. Place the beef and vegetable mixture over the potatoes, and top with remaining potatoes.
5. Cook, covered, 45 minutes in the preheated oven, or until the potatoes are tender.

QUICK BRUSCHETTA CHICKEN BAKE

Servings: 6 | Prep: 20m | Cooks: 30m | Total: 50m

NUTRITION FACTS

Calories: 349 | Carbohydrates: 25.9g | Fat: 8.5g | Protein: 39.2g | Cholesterol: 90mg

INGREDIENTS

- 1 1/2 pounds skinless, boneless chicken breast halves - cubed
- 1 tablespoon minced garlic
- 1 teaspoon salt
- 1 (6 ounce) box chicken-flavored dry bread stuffing mix
- 1 (15 ounce) can diced tomatoes with juice
- 2 cups shredded mozzarella cheese
- 1/2 cup water
- 1 tablespoon Italian seasoning

DIRECTIONS

1. Preheat oven to 400 degrees F (200 degrees C). Spray a 9x13-inch glass baking dish with cooking spray.
2. Toss the cubed chicken with the salt in a large bowl. Place the chicken in a layer into the bottom of the baking dish. Stir together tomatoes, water, garlic, and stuffing mix in a large bowl; set aside to soften. Sprinkle the cheese on top of the chicken, then sprinkle with the Italian seasoning. Spread the softened stuffing mixture on top.

3. Bake uncovered until the chicken cubes have turned white and are no longer pink in the center, about 30 minutes.

WHIT'S CHICKEN ENCHILADAS

Servings: 8 | Prep: 30m | Cooks: 30m | Total: 1h

NUTRITION FACTS

Calories: 706 | Carbohydrates: 38.7g | Fat: 44g | Protein: 38.1g | Cholesterol: 160mg

INGREDIENTS

- 4 bone-in chicken breast halves
- 1 (8 ounce) package cream cheese
- 2 tablespoons olive oil
- 2 cups shredded Monterey Jack cheese, divided
- 1 (4 ounce) can diced green chile peppers, drained
- 1/2 cup water
- 1 jalapeno pepper, chopped
- 8 (10 inch) flour tortillas
- 1 clove garlic, minced
- 1 cup heavy cream

DIRECTIONS

1. Place the chicken breast halves into a saucepan, and fill with enough water to cover. Bring to a boil, and cook until the chicken is cooked through, about 20 minutes. Remove from the water, and set aside to cool.
2. Preheat the oven to 375 degrees F (190 degrees C). Remove the chicken meat from the breasts, and discard the skin and bones. Set aside.
3. Heat the olive oil in a large skillet over medium heat. Add the green chilies, jalapeno and garlic. Cook and stir for a few minutes, until fragrant, then stir in the cream cheese and half of the Monterey Jack. As the cheese begins to melt, gradually stir in the water. Chop the chicken meat, and stir into the skillet. Remove from the heat.
4. Spoon the chicken mixture into tortillas, and roll up. Place the rolls seam side down in a 9x13 inch baking dish. Sprinkle the remaining Monterey Jack cheese over the top, then pour cream over all.
5. Bake for 30 minutes in the preheated oven, or until the enchiladas are golden brown on the top.

HEAVENLY POTATOES AND HAM

Servings: 12 | Prep: 30m | Cooks: 30m | Total: 1h

NUTRITION FACTS

Calories: 506 | Carbohydrates: 43.3g | Fat: 30.1g | Protein: 15.9g | Cholesterol: 82mg

INGREDIENTS

- 5 pounds red potatoes, quartered
- 1/4 cup chopped green onion
- 1 (16 ounce) container sour cream
- 2 cups cooked, chopped ham
- 1/2 cup butter
- salt and pepper to taste
- 1 (10.75 ounce) can condensed cream of chicken soup
- 1 1/2 cups Parmesan cheese flavored bread crumbs
- 2 cups shredded Cheddar cheese
- 1/4 cup melted butter

DIRECTIONS

1. Preheat oven to 350 degrees F (175 degrees C). Lightly grease a 9x13 inch baking dish.
2. Place potatoes in a large pot of water, and bring to a boil. Boil until slightly tender, about 12 minutes. Drain, and transfer to a large bowl.
3. Mix sour cream, butter, cream of chicken soup, Cheddar cheese, green onions, ham, salt and pepper with the potatoes. Spread mixture in the prepared baking dish. Sprinkle with bread crumbs, and drizzle with butter.
4. Bake 30 minutes in the preheated oven.

SOUR CREAM CHICKEN ENCHILADAS

Servings: 12 | Prep: 20m | Cooks: 30m | Total: 50m

NUTRITION FACTS

Calories: 265 | Carbohydrates: 22.8g | Fat: 13.3g | Protein: 13.1g | Cholesterol: 40mg

INGREDIENTS

- 1 bunch cilantro
- 2 skinless, boneless chicken breast halves, cooked and shredded
- 1 cup sour cream
- 1 onion
- 2 (7 ounce) cans jalapeno salsa
- 12 (6 inch) flour tortillas
- 2 (7 ounce) cans prepared green chile salsa
- 2 cups shredded Cheddar cheese

DIRECTIONS

1. To Make Sour Cream Mixture: In a blender or food processor, puree cilantro, sour cream, jalapeno salsa and 1/2 can of the green chile salsa. Set aside.
2. To Make Chicken Mixture: In a large bowl, combine shredded chicken, onion and the remaining 1 1/2 cans of green chile salsa. Mix well.
3. Preheat oven to 350 degrees F (175 degrees C).
4. Heat tortillas in conventional or microwave oven until soft. Pour enough of the sour cream mixture into a 9x13 inch baking dish to coat the bottom. Place 2 heaping tablespoonfuls of the chicken mixture in each tortilla, roll up and place seam side down in the baking dish. Pour remaining sour cream mixture over all and top with shredded cheese.
5. Cover dish tightly with aluminum foil and bake at 350 degrees F (175 degrees C) for about 30 minutes, or until dish is heated through and bubbling.

ITALIAN MEATBALL SANDWICH CASSEROLE
Servings: 5 | Prep: 30m | Cooks: 30m | Total: 1h

NUTRITION FACTS

Calories: 1046 | Carbohydrates: 74.3g | Fat: 64.4g | Protein: 40.8g | Cholesterol: 153mg

INGREDIENTS

- 1/3 cup chopped green onions
- 1 teaspoon Italian seasoning
- 1/4 cup Italian seasoned bread crumbs
- 1/4 teaspoon freshly ground black pepper
- 3 tablespoons grated Parmesan cheese
- 2 cups shredded mozzarella cheese
- 1 pound ground beef
- 3 cups spaghetti sauce
- 1 (1 pound) loaf Italian bread, cut into 1-inch cubes
- 1 cup water
- 1 (8 ounce) package cream cheese, softened
- 2 cloves garlic, minced
- 1/2 cup mayonnaise

DIRECTIONS

1. Preheat oven to 400 degrees F (205 degrees C).
2. Mix together onions, bread crumbs, Parmesan cheese and ground beef. Roll into 1 inch diameter balls, and place in a baking pan. Bake for 15 to 20 minutes, or until beef is no longer pink. Reduce the oven temperature to 350 degrees F (175 degrees C).

3. Arrange the bread cubes in a single layer in an ungreased 9x13 inch baking dish. Mix together the cream cheese, mayonnaise, Italian seasoning and black pepper until smooth. Spread this mixture over each bread cube. Sprinkle with 1/2 cup of the grated mozzarella cheese.
4. In a large bowl, mix together spaghetti sauce, water, and garlic. Gently stir in meatballs. Pour over the bread and cheese mixture in the baking pan. Sprinkle the remaining mozzarella cheese evenly over the top.
5. Bake at 350 degrees F (175 degrees C) for 30 minutes, or until heated through.

QUICK AND EASY TUNA CASSEROLE
Servings: 5 | Prep: 5m | Cooks: 25m | Total: 30m

NUTRITION FACTS

Calories: 662 | Carbohydrates: 71.8g | Fat: 24.2g | Protein: 38.4g | Cholesterol: 112mg

INGREDIENTS

- 1 (12 ounce) package egg noodles
- 1 onion, chopped
- 2 cups frozen green peas
- 10 slices American processed cheese
- 2 (10.75 ounce) cans condensed cream of mushroom soup
- ground black pepper to taste
- 2 (5 ounce) cans tuna, drained

DIRECTIONS

1. Bring a large pot of water to a boil. Add noodles and frozen peas. Cook until noodles are al dente, drain well. Return noodles and peas to the pot.
2. Mix soup, tuna fish, onions, processed cheese and pepper into the pot. Stir constantly until all of the ingredients are well mixed and the cheese has melted. Serve.

BEEF BOURGUIGNON
Servings: 4 | Prep: 20m | Cooks: 3h | Total: 3h20m

NUTRITION FACTS

Calories: 583 | Carbohydrates: 21.9g | Fat: 31g | Protein: 32.2g | Cholesterol: 125mg

INGREDIENTS

- 1/4 cup all-purpose flour
- 1 clove garlic, minced
- 1 teaspoon salt

- 2 cups red wine
- 1/2 teaspoon ground black pepper
- 1 bay leaf
- 2 pounds cubed stew meat
- 3 tablespoons chopped fresh parsley
- 4 tablespoons butter
- 1/2 teaspoon dried thyme
- 1 onion, chopped
- 1 (6 ounce) can sliced mushrooms
- 2 carrots, chopped
- 1 (16 ounce) can canned onions

DIRECTIONS

1. In a small bowl, combine the flour, salt and ground black pepper. Coat the beef cubes with this mixture.
2. Melt the butter or margarine in a large skillet over medium high heat. Add the meat and brown well on all sides. Pour this into a 2 quart casserole dish.
3. Return the skillet to the heat and add the onion, carrots and garlic to it. Saute for 5 to 10 minutes, or until onion is tender. add the wine, bay leaf, parsley, thyme, and liquid from the mushrooms. Pour over meat.
4. Bake, covered, at 350 degrees F (175 degrees C) for 2 1/2 hours. Remove cover, add canned onions and mushroom crowns, and bake for 30 more minutes

NO-NOODLE ZUCCHINI LASAGNA

Servings: 8 | Prep: 30m | Cooks: 1h | Total: 1h30m

NUTRITION FACTS

Calories: 494 | Carbohydrates: 23.2g | Fat: 27.3g | Protein: 41.3g | Cholesterol: 118mg

INGREDIENTS

- 2 large zucchini
- 1 tablespoon chopped fresh oregano
- 1 tablespoon salt
- hot water as needed
- 1 pound ground beef
- 1 egg
- 1 1/2 teaspoons ground black pepper
- 1 (15 ounce) container low-fat ricotta cheese
- 1 small green bell pepper, diced
- 2 tablespoons chopped fresh parsley

- 1 onion, diced
- 1 (16 ounce) package frozen chopped spinach, thawed and drained
- 1 cup tomato paste
- 1 pound fresh mushrooms, sliced
- 1 (16 ounce) can tomato sauce
- 8 ounces shredded mozzarella cheese
- 1/4 cup red wine
- 8 ounces grated Parmesan cheese
- 2 tablespoons chopped fresh basil

DIRECTIONS

1. Preheat oven to 325 degrees F (165 degrees C). Grease a deep 9x13 inch baking pan.
2. Slice zucchini lengthwise into very thin slices. Sprinkle slices lightly with salt; set aside to drain in a colander.
3. To prepare the meat sauce, cook and stir ground beef and black pepper in a large skillet over medium high heat for 5 minutes. Add in green pepper and onion; cook and stir until meat is no longer pink. Stir in tomato paste, tomato sauce, wine, basil, and oregano, adding a small amount of hot water if sauce is too thick. Bring to a boil; reduce heat and simmer sauce for about 20 minutes, stirring frequently.
4. Meanwhile, stir egg, ricotta, and parsley together in a bowl until well combined.
5. To assemble lasagna, spread 1/2 of the meat sauce into the bottom of prepared pan. Then layer 1/2 the zucchini slices, 1/2 the ricotta mixture, all of the spinach, followed by all of the mushrooms, then 1/2 the mozzarella cheese. Repeat by layering the remaining meat sauce, zucchini slices, ricotta mixture, and mozzarella. Spread Parmesan cheese evenly over the top; cover with foil.
6. Bake for 45 minutes. Remove foil; raise oven temperature to 350 degrees F (175 degrees C), and bake an additional 15 minutes. Let stand for 5 minutes before serving.

AWESOME BAKED SEA SCALLOPS
Servings: 4 | Prep: 10m | Cooks: 14m | Total: 24m

NUTRITION FACTS

Calories: 440 | Carbohydrates: 29.8g | Fat: 30.2g | Protein: 15.2g | Cholesterol: 58mg

INGREDIENTS

- 16 sea scallops, rinsed and drained
- salt and pepper to taste
- 5 tablespoons butter, melted
- 1 cup bread crumbs
- 5 cloves garlic, minced
- 4 tablespoons olive oil

- 2 shallots, chopped
- 1/4 cup chopped parsley
- 3 pinches ground nutmeg
- lemon wedges for garnish (optional)

DIRECTIONS

1. Preheat oven to 425 degrees F (220 degrees C).
2. Place scallops, melted butter, garlic, and shallots in a bowl. Season with nutmeg, salt, and pepper. Stir gently to combine. Transfer to a casserole dish.
3. In a separate bowl, combine bread crumbs and olive oil. Sprinkle on top of scallops.
4. Bake in preheated oven until crumbs are brown and scallops are done, about 11 to 14 minutes. Top with parsley, and serve with lemon wedges on the side.

TUNA NOODLE CASSEROLE

Servings: 8 | Prep: 10m | Cooks: 50m | Total: 1h

NUTRITION FACTS

Calories: 467 | Carbohydrates: 57.6g | Fat: 16g | Protein: 22.6g | Cholesterol: 30mg

INGREDIENTS

- 1 (16 ounce) package uncooked pasta shells
- 1 teaspoon salt
- 2 (5 ounce) cans tuna, drained
- 1/4 teaspoon ground black pepper
- 1 (10.75 ounce) can condensed cream of mushroom soup
- 1 teaspoon crushed garlic
- 1 (10.75 ounce) can condensed cream of celery soup
- 4 slices processed American cheese
- 1 1/4 cups milk
- 1 1/2 cups crushed potato chips

DIRECTIONS

1. Boil pasta in lightly salted water for 10 minutes, or until al dente; drain well. Return the pasta to the pot it was cooked in.
2. Preheat oven to 350 degrees F (175 degrees C). Spray a 2 1/2 quart casserole dish with cooking spray.
3. Mix tuna with cream of mushroom soup, cream of celery soup, milk, salt, black pepper, and garlic in a medium saucepan. Place pan over medium low heat, and heat through. Alternatively, place these ingredients in a microwave safe dish, and warm in the microwave.

4. Mix tuna mixture with pasta. Spread 1/2 of the noodles into the prepared dish. Arrange the cheese slices over the noodles, then spread the remaining noodle mixture over the cheese. Top with crushed potato chips.

5. Bake, uncovered, for 20 to 30 minutes; cook until the casserole is hot, and the chips begin to brown. Let cool for 10 minutes before serving.

HEARTY HAM CASSEROLE

Servings: 5 | Prep: 45m | Cooks: 35m | Total: 1h20m

NUTRITION FACTS

Calories: 452 | Carbohydrates: 33g | Fat: 27.4g | Protein: 21g | Cholesterol: 76mg

INGREDIENTS

- 2 cups potatoes, cubed
- 1 tablespoon chopped onions
- 2 cups cooked ham, cubed
- 1/3 cup all-purpose flour
- 1 (15.25 ounce) can whole kernel corn, drained
- 1 3/4 cups milk
- 1/4 cup finely minced fresh parsley
- 1/8 teaspoon ground black pepper
- 1/4 cup butter
- 4 ounces processed cheese food, shredded

DIRECTIONS

1. Preheat oven to 350 degrees F (175 degrees C).
2. Bring a large pot of salted water to a boil. Add potatoes and cook until tender but still firm, about 15 minutes. Drain and cool.
3. Combine potatoes, ham, corn and parsley; set aside. In a saucepan saute onion in butter for 2 minutes, stir in flour until blended well. Gradually add milk and pepper. Bring to a boil. Cook and stir for 2 minutes. Remove from heat and pour over the ham mixture. Stir to mix well.
4. Pour into greased 11x7 baking dish. Cover and bake for 25 minutes. Uncover, sprinkle with cheese and bake 5 to 10 minutes longer until cheese melts.

SWISS CHICKEN CASSEROLE

Servings: 6 | Prep: 10m | Cooks: 50m | Total: 1h

NUTRITION FACTS

Calories: 568 | Carbohydrates: 34.1g | Fat: 29.1g | Protein: 40.7g | Cholesterol: 140mg

INGREDIENTS

- 6 skinless, boneless chicken breast halves
- 1/4 cup milk
- 6 slices Swiss cheese
- 1 (8 ounce) package dry bread stuffing mix
- 1 (10.75 ounce) can condensed cream of chicken soup
- ½ cup melted butter

DIRECTIONS

1. Preheat oven to 350 degrees F (175 degrees C). Lightly grease a 9x13 inch baking dish.
2. Arrange chicken breasts in the baking dish. Place one slice of Swiss cheese on top of each chicken breast. Combine cream of chicken soup and milk in a medium bowl, and pour over chicken breasts. Sprinkle with stuffing mix. Pour melted butter over top, and cover with foil.
3. Bake 50 minutes, or until chicken is no longer pink and juices run clear.

EASY FRENCH TOAST CASSEROLE

Servings: 8 | Prep: 15m | Cooks: 35m | Total: 8h50m

NUTRITION FACTS

Calories: 382 | Carbohydrates: 48.1g | Fat: 17g | Protein: 10.2g | Cholesterol: 175mg

INGREDIENTS

- 1 cup brown sugar
- 6 eggs
- 1/2 cup butter
- 2 teaspoons vanilla extract
- 1 (8 ounce) loaf crusty French bread, cut into bite-size pieces, or as needed
- 1 pinch ground cinnamon, or to taste
- 2 cups milk
- 1 tablespoon brown sugar, or as needed

DIRECTIONS

1. Grease a 9x12-inch baking dish.
2. Stir 1 cup brown sugar and butter together in a saucepan over medium-low heat until butter melts and sugar dissolves into butter, 2 to 4 minutes. Pour into prepared baking dish and spread a 1 1/2- to 2-inch layer of bread pieces over the top.
3. Beat milk, eggs, and vanilla extract together in a bowl; pour milk mixture over bread into the baking dish and move bread as necessary to ensure all bread is absorbing liquid. Sprinkle cinnamon over the top. Cover the dish with plastic wrap and refrigerate, 8 hours to overnight.

4. Preheat oven to 450 degrees F (230 degrees C). Remove and discard plastic wrap from baking dish and sprinkle remaining brown sugar over the top of the bread mixture.
5. Bake in the preheated oven until browned and bubbling, about 30 minutes.

HOT TAMALE PIE

Servings: 8 | Prep: 20m | Cooks: 1h10m | Total: 1h30m

NUTRITION FACTS

Calories: 640 | Carbohydrates: 54.3g | Fat: 31.8g | Protein: 34.7g | Cholesterol: 146mg

INGREDIENTS

- cooking spray
- 2 (8.5 ounce) boxes dry corn muffin mix (such as Jiffy®)
- 2 pounds ground beef
- 2 eggs
- 2 cups diced poblano peppers
- 2/3 cup milk, divided
- 1 teaspoon salt
- 4 ounces shredded Cheddar cheese, divided
- 1 (16 ounce) jar salsa
- 4 ounces shredded Monterey Jack cheese, divided
- 1/2 teaspoon dried oregano
- 8 ounces frozen corn, thawed
- 1 teaspoon ground dried chipotle pepper

DIRECTIONS

1. Preheat the oven to 350 degrees F (175 degrees C).
2. Spray a 9x13-inch casserole dish with cooking spray.
3. Cook and stir ground beef in a Dutch oven over medium-high heat until meat starts to brown and release juices, about 5 minutes.
4. Reduce heat to medium and stir in poblano peppers, salt, salsa, oregano, and chipotle powder; cook and stir until seasoned beef is crumbly and no longer pink, about 10 minutes.
5. Mix one package of corn muffin mix in a large bowl with 1 egg and 1/3 cup of milk. Whisk to combine. In a separate large bowl, mix the second package of corn muffin mix with 1 egg, 1/3 cup of milk and half the Cheddar and Monterey Jack cheeses.
6. Spread the prepared corn muffin mixture without cheese into the prepared baking dish. Sprinkle corn over the muffin mix, followed by remaining half of the cheeses, then the beef mixture.
7. Spoon the corn muffin mix with cheese on top of the beef and carefully spread over the top with a fork, leaving about half an inch from the edges of the pan.
8. Bake in the preheated oven for 50-60 minutes, until golden brown.

BISCUITS AND GRAVY CASSEROLE

Servings: 6 | Prep: 10m | Cooks: 35m | Total: 45m

NUTRITION FACTS

Calories: 688 | Carbohydrates: 27.3g | Fat: 52.2g | Protein: 26.6g | Cholesterol: 270mg

INGREDIENTS

- 1 (10 ounce) can refrigerated biscuit dough (such as Pillsbury Grands!®)
- 1/2 cup milk
- 1 (1 pound) bulk pork sausage
- salt and ground black pepper to taste
- 1 1/2 cups shredded Cheddar cheese, divided
- 1 1/2 cups cold water, or more as needed
- 6 eggs
- 1 (1.5 ounce) package pork gravy mix

DIRECTIONS

1. Preheat oven to 350 degrees F (175 degrees C). Grease a 9x13-inch baking dish.
2. Line the bottom of the prepared baking dish with biscuits.
3. Heat a large skillet over medium-high heat. Cook and stir sausage in the hot skillet until browned and crumbly, 5 to 7 minutes; drain and discard grease. Scatter sausage over biscuit layer and top with 1 cup Cheddar cheese
4. Whisk eggs, milk, salt, and pepper together in a bowl and pour over cheese layer.
5. Mix water and gravy mix together in a saucepan; bring to a boil. Reduce heat and simmer until gravy is thickened, 1 to 2 minutes, adding more water for a thinner gravy. Pour gravy over egg layer. Sprinkle remaining 1/2 cup Cheddar cheese over casserole.
6. Bake in the preheated oven until egg is fluffy and cheese is bubbling, about 30 minutes.

BAKED SPAGHETTI SQUASH WITH BEEF AND VEGGIES

Servings: 6 | Prep: 25m | Cooks: 1h25m | Total: 1h50m

NUTRITION FACTS

Calories: 399 | Carbohydrates: 12.8g | Fat: 26.4g | Protein: 27.2g | Cholesterol: 100mg

INGREDIENTS

- 1 spaghetti squash, halved and seeded
- 1/2 teaspoon dried oregano
- 1 pound ground beef
- 1/2 teaspoon dried basil

- 1/2 cup diced green bell pepper
- 1/4 teaspoon salt
- 1/2 cup diced red bell pepper
- 1/4 teaspoon ground black pepper
- 1/4 cup diced red onion
- 2 1/4 cups shredded sharp Cheddar cheese
- 1 clove garlic, chopped
- 1 (14.5 ounce) can Italian-style diced tomatoes, drained

DIRECTIONS

1. Preheat oven to 375 degrees F (190 degrees C).
2. Place squash on a baking sheet, and bake 40 minutes, or until tender. Remove from heat, cool, and shred pulp with a fork.
3. Reduce oven temperature to 350 degrees F (175 degrees C). Lightly grease a casserole dish.
4. In a skillet over medium heat, cook the ground beef until evenly brown. Drain, and mix in the green pepper, red pepper, red onion, and garlic. Continue to cook and stir until vegetables are tender.
5. Mix the shredded squash and tomatoes into the skillet, and season with oregano, basil, salt, and pepper. Cook and stir until heated through. Remove skillet from heat, and mix in 2 cups cheese until melted. Transfer to the prepared casserole dish.
6. Bake 25 minutes in the preheated oven. Sprinkle with remaining cheese, and continue baking 5 minutes, until cheese is melted.

TATER TOT CASSEROLE

Servings: 5 | Prep: 10m | Cooks: 25m | Total: 35m

NUTRITION FACTS

Calories: 356 | Carbohydrates: 26.5g | Fat: 21g | Protein: 17.8g | Cholesterol: 59mg

INGREDIENTS

- 1 pound ground beef
- 1 tablespoon ketchup
- 1 medium onion, chopped
- 1 tablespoon Worcestershire sauce
- 1 (10.75 ounce) can Campbell's® Condensed Cream of Mushroom Soup (Regular or 98% Fat Free)
- 3 cups frozen Tater Tots

DIRECTIONS

1. Cook beef and onion in 10-inch skillet over medium-high heat until beef is well browned, stirring to break up meat. Pour off fat.

2. Stir soup, ketchup and Worcestershire into skillet. Spoon beef mixture into 12x8-inch shallow baking dish. Arrange potatoes around edge of casserole.
3. Bake at 425 degrees F for 25 minutes or until potatoes are done.

GROUND TURKEY CASSEROLE

Servings: 8 | Prep: 30m | Cooks: 35m | Total: 1h5m

NUTRITION FACTS

Calories: 516 | Carbohydrates: 31.8g | Fat: 31.5g | Protein: 26.9g | Cholesterol: 145mg

INGREDIENTS

- 1 pound ground turkey
- 1 (8 ounce) package cream cheese
- 1 (15 ounce) can tomato sauce
- 1 (12 ounce) package uncooked egg noodles
- 1 teaspoon white sugar
- 2 cups shredded Cheddar cheese
- 1 (8 ounce) container sour cream

DIRECTIONS

1. Preheat oven to 350 degrees F (175 degrees C).
2. In a large skillet over medium-high heat, saute the ground turkey for 5 to 10 minutes, or until browned. Drain the turkey, stir in the tomato sauce and sugar, and set aside. In a medium bowl, combine the sour cream and cream cheese. Mix well and set aside.
3. Cook noodles according to package directions. Place them into a 9x13-inch baking dish, then layer the turkey mixture over the noodles. Then layer the sour cream mixture over the turkey, and top with cheese.
4. Bake at 350 degrees F (175 degrees C) for 20 to 35 minutes, or until cheese is melted and bubbly.

GROUND TURKEY CASSEROLE

Servings: 12 | Prep: 30m | Cooks: 30m | Total: 1h

NUTRITION FACTS

Calories: 383 | Carbohydrates: 21.8g | Fat: 22.9g | Protein: 22.4g | Cholesterol: 71mg

INGREDIENTS

- 1 pound lean ground beef
- 1 (12 ounce) package corn tortillas
- 1 (15 ounce) can ranch-style beans

- 4 cups shredded Cheddar cheese
- 1 (14.5 ounce) can peeled and diced tomatoes
- 2 tablespoons chili powder
- 1 (10.75 ounce) can condensed cream of mushroom soup

DIRECTIONS

1. Preheat oven to 350 degrees F (175 degrees C).
2. Brown the ground beef in a large skillet over medium high heat. Add chili powder, beans, tomatoes and soup; mix well and heat thoroughly.
3. Line a 13x9 inch dish with tortillas. Then make a layer with the meat mixture. Make another row of tortillas, then finish off with rest of meat mixture. Top with grated cheese.
4. Bake in a preheated oven for 30 minutes.

DELICIOUS CHICKEN CASSEROLE

Servings: 8 | Prep: 15m | Cooks: 1h15m | Total: 1h30m

NUTRITION FACTS

Calories: 385 | Carbohydrates: 21.1g | Fat: g | Protein: 16.3g | Cholesterol: 79mg

INGREDIENTS

- 4 skinless, bone-in chicken breast halves
- 1/4 teaspoon celery salt
- 2 stalks celery, cut into thirds
- 1/8 teaspoon onion powder
- 1/2 teaspoon salt
- 1/4 teaspoon garlic powder
- 1/8 teaspoon pepper
- salt and pepper to taste
- 1 cup cooked rice
- 2 cups crushed buttery round crackers
- 6 ounces sour cream
- 1/2 cup butter or margarine, melted
- 2 (10.5 ounce) cans condensed cream of chicken soup

DIRECTIONS

1. Preheat oven to 350 degrees F (175 degrees C).
2. Bring to a boil the chicken breasts, celery, 1/2 teaspoon salt, 1/8 teaspoon pepper, and enough water to cover. Cover, reduce heat to medium low; simmer for 35 minutes. Drain, reserving 1 cup liquid. Cool chicken, remove meat from bones, and cut into bite-size pieces.

3. In a large bowl, stir together sour cream, soup, broth, celery salt, onion powder, garlic powder, and salt and pepper to taste. Mix in cooked rice and chicken. Spoon mixture into a 9x13 inch casserole dish. In a resealable bag, shake together crushed crackers and melted butter. Sprinkle crackers over the top.

4. Bake in preheated oven for 30 to 35 minutes.

TACO LASAGNA

Servings: 12 | Prep: 20m | Cooks: 45m | Total: 1h15m | Additional: 10m

NUTRITION FACTS

Calories: 475 | Carbohydrates: 28.2g | Fat: 28.5g | Protein: 26.7g | Cholesterol: 97mg

INGREDIENTS

- 2 pounds lean ground beef
- 18 (6 inch) corn tortillas
- 2 (1.25 ounce) packages taco seasoning mix
- 1 (24 ounce) jar salsa
- 4 cloves garlic, minced
- 1 cup sliced green onion
- 1/2 teaspoon cayenne pepper
- 1 (16 ounce) container sour cream
- 1 tablespoon chili powder
- 1 1/2 cups shredded Cheddar cheese
- 1/2 cup water
- 1 1/2 cups shredded Monterey Jack cheese

DIRECTIONS

1. Place ground beef in a large, deep skillet. Cook over medium high heat until evenly brown. Drain, then season with taco seasoning, garlic, cayenne pepper, chili powder and water. Simmer for 10 minutes.

2. Preheat oven to 375 degrees F (190 degrees C). Grease the bottom of a 9x13 inch baking dish.

3. Place 6 tortillas into the prepared baking dish. Spread 1/3 of the salsa on top of the tortillas. Spread 1/2 of the meat mixture evenly over the salsa. Sprinkle with 1/2 of the green onions. Drop 1/2 of the sour cream randomly over the green onions. Top with 1/2 cup Cheddar and 1/2 cup Monterey Jack cheese. Repeat layers. Top with 6 tortillas, spread with remaining salsa, and sprinkle with remaining cheese.

4. Bake in a preheated oven for 30 to 45 minutes or until cheeses are melted.

CREAMY POTATO PORK CHOP BAKE

Servings: 6 | Prep: 15m | Cooks: 45m | Total: 1h

NUTRITION FACTS

Calories: 720 | Carbohydrates: 46.4g | Fat: 55.3g | Protein: 18.9g | Cholesterol: 69mg

INGREDIENTS

- 1 tablespoon vegetable oil
- salt and pepper to taste
- 6 pork chops
- 1 (20 ounce) package frozen hash brown potatoes, thawed
- 1 (10.75 ounce) can condensed cream of celery soup
- 1 cup shredded Cheddar cheese
- 1/2 cup milk
- 1 1/2 cups French-fried onions, divided
- 1/2 cup sour cream

DIRECTIONS

1. Heat oil in a large skillet over medium high heat. Add pork chops and saute until browned. Remove from skillet and drain on paper toweling.
2. Meanwhile, preheat oven to 350 degrees F (175 degrees C)
3. In a medium bowl mix together soup, milk, sour cream and salt and pepper to taste. Stir in potatoes, 1/2 cup cheese and 1/2 cup onions. Mix together and spread mixture in the bottom of a 9x13 inch baking dish. Arrange pork chops over potato mixture.
4. Cover dish and bake in the preheated oven for about 40 minutes, or until internal temperature of pork has reached 145 degrees F (63 degrees C). Remove cover; top with remaining cheese and onions and bake uncovered for 5 more minutes.

ENCHILADA CASSEROLE

Servings: 8 | Prep: 20m | Cooks: 35m | Total: 1h | Additional: 5m

NUTRITION FACTS

Calories: 449 | Carbohydrates: 34.6g | Fat: 22g | Protein: 28.4g | Cholesterol: 87mg

INGREDIENTS

- 1 (1.5 ounce) package dry enchilada sauce mix
- 1/2 teaspoon onion powder
- 1 (6 ounce) can tomato paste
- 1 (16 ounce) can refried beans

- 3/4 cup water
- 1 (12 ounce) package corn tortillas
- 1 1/2 pounds ground beef
- 1 cup shredded Cheddar cheese
- 1 teaspoon garlic salt
- 1 cup shredded Monterey Jack cheese

DIRECTIONS

1. Preheat oven to 375 degrees F (190 degrees C).
2. In a medium bowl, mix the dry enchilada sauce according to package directions, replacing tomato sauce with the tomato paste and water
3. In a large skillet, brown the ground beef with garlic salt and onion powder; drain fat. Mix refried beans and 1/2 cup of the prepared enchilada sauce with the meat.
4. Dip enough corn tortillas to cover the bottom of a 3 quart casserole dish in the remaining enchilada sauce. Arrange tortillas in the dish. Spoon in half of the meat mixture, covering the tortillas. Spread half of the Cheddar and Monterey Jack cheeses over the meat. Cover with another layer tortillas dipped in enchilada sauce. Spoon in remaining meat mixture and top with a final layer of tortillas dipped in enchilada sauce. Pour any remaining sauce over the layers and top with remaining cheese.
5. Cover and bake in preheated oven for 20 minutes. Remove from oven and let sit for 5 minutes before serving.

BROWN RICE AND BLACK BEAN CASSEROLE
Servings: 8 | Prep: 15m | Cooks: 1h35m | Total: 1h50m

NUTRITION FACTS

Calories: 337 | Carbohydrates: 11.5g | Fat: 21g | Protein: 25.3g | Cholesterol: 77mg

INGREDIENTS

- 1/3 cup brown rice
- 1/2 teaspoon cumin
- 1 cup vegetable broth
- salt to taste
- 1 tablespoon olive oil
- ground cayenne pepper to taste
- 1/3 cup diced onion
- 1 (15 ounce) can black beans, drained
- 1 medium zucchini, thinly sliced
- 1 (4 ounce) can diced green chile peppers, drained
- 2 cooked skinless boneless chicken breast halves, chopped
- 1/3 cup shredded carrots

- 1/2 cup sliced mushrooms
- 2 cups shredded Swiss cheese

DIRECTIONS

1. Mix the rice and vegetable broth in a pot, and bring to a boil. Reduce heat to low, cover, and simmer 45 minutes, or until rice is tender.
2. Preheat oven to 350 degrees F (175 degrees C). Lightly grease a large casserole dish.
3. Heat the olive oil in a skillet over medium heat, and cook the onion until tender. Mix in the zucchini, chicken, and mushrooms. Season with cumin, salt, and ground cayenne pepper. Cook and stir until zucchini is lightly browned and chicken is heated through.
4. In large bowl, mix the cooked rice, onion, zucchini, chicken, mushrooms, beans, chiles, carrots, and 1/2 the Swiss cheese. Transfer to the prepared casserole dish, and sprinkle with remaining cheese.
5. Cover casserole loosely with foil, and bake 30 minutes in the preheated oven. Uncover, and continue baking 10 minutes, or until bubbly and lightly browned.

CHICKEN SUIZA CORNBREAD BAKE
Servings: 12 | Prep: 20m | Cooks: 40m | Total: 1h

NUTRITION FACTS

Calories: 378 | Carbohydrates: 30.1g | Fat: 21.8g | Protein: 17.9g | Cholesterol: 70mg

INGREDIENTS

- 1/2 cup butter
- 2 1/3 cups chopped cooked chicken breast
- 1 onion, finely chopped
- 2 tablespoons canned green chile peppers, chopped
- 1 clove garlic, minced
- 4 ounces sliced fresh mushrooms
- 1 (15.25 ounce) can whole kernel corn, drained
- 1 1/2 cups reduced-fat sour cream
- 1 (15 ounce) can cream-style corn, drained
- 1/4teaspoon salt, or to taste
- 1/4teaspoon salt
- 1/4 teaspoon ground black pepper, or to taste
- 1/2 cup egg substitute
- 1 (8 ounce) package Monterey Jack cheese, shredded
- 1 (8.5 ounce) package corn bread mix

DIRECTIONS

1. Preheat oven to 375 degrees F (190 degrees C). Grease a 9x13-inch baking dish.

2. Melt butter in a small skillet over medium heat. Add onion and garlic; cook and stir until tender, 4 to 6 minutes (see Cook's Note). Remove from heat and set aside. In a large bowl, combine corn, cream-style corn, salt, and egg substitute. Beat in muffin mix. Fold in cooked onion mixture. Pour into prepared baking dish.
3. In a large bowl, combine chicken, green chiles, mushrooms, sour cream, salt and pepper. Spoon over corn mixture to within 1 inch from edge. Sprinkle top with cheese.
4. Bake in preheated oven for 35 to 40 minutes, or until edges are golden brown.

BUSY DAY CHICKEN RICE CASSEROLE

Servings: 8 | Prep: 10m | Cooks: 2h | Total: 2h10m

NUTRITION FACTS

Calories: 291 | Carbohydrates: 27.7g | Fat: 5.7g | Protein: 30.5g | Cholesterol: 73mg

INGREDIENTS

- 1 (10.75 ounce) can condensed cream of mushroom soup
- 1 pinch garlic powder
- 1 (10.75 ounce) can condensed cream of celery soup
- ground black pepper to taste
- 1 cup water
- 1 (1 ounce) package dry onion soup mix
- 1 cup uncooked white rice
- 8 skinless, boneless chicken breast halves
- 1 (4.5 ounce) can mushrooms, drained

DIRECTIONS

1. Preheat oven to 325 degrees F (165 degrees C).
2. In a large bowl combine the mushroom soup, celery soup, water, rice, mushrooms, garlic powder and black pepper. Mix all together. Pour mixture into a 9x13 inch baking dish and spread on bottom.
3. Lay chicken pieces over soup mixture and sprinkle dry onion soup mix over all. Cover tightly with aluminum foil and bake in the preheated oven for 1 to 1 1/2 hours or until chicken is cooked through and no longer pink inside.

CHRISTMAS BRUNCH CASSEROLE

Servings: 5 | Prep: 40m | Cooks: 1h | Total: 1d | Additional: 1d

NUTRITION FACTS

Calories: 494 | Carbohydrates: 31.9g | Fat: 28.6g | Protein: 28.1g | Cholesterol: 217mg

INGREDIENTS

- 1 pound bacon
- 1/4 teaspoon garlic salt
- 2 onions, chopped
- 1/2 teaspoon ground black pepper
- 2 cups fresh sliced mushrooms
- 4 eggs
- 1 tablespoon butter
- 1 1/2 cups milk
- 4 cups frozen hash brown potatoes, thawed
- 1 pinch dried parsley
- 1 teaspoon salt
- 1 cup shredded Cheddar cheess

DIRECTIONS

1. Place bacon in a large skillet. Cook over medium-high heat until evenly brown. Drain and set aside. Add the mushrooms and onion to the skillet; cook and stir until the onion has softened and turned translucent and the mushrooms are tender, about 5 minutes.
2. Grease a 9x13-inch casserole dish with the tablespoon of butter. Place potatoes in bottom of prepared dish. Sprinkle with salt, garlic salt, and pepper. Top with crumbled bacon, then add the onions and mushrooms.
3. In a mixing bowl, beat the eggs with the milk and parsley. Pour the beaten eggs over the casserole and top with grated cheese. Cover and refrigerate overnight.
4. Preheat oven to 400 degrees F (200 degrees C).
5. Bake in preheated oven for 1 hour or until set.

PORK CHOP AND POTATO CASSEROLE

Servings: 5 | Prep: 20m | Cooks: 1h | Total: 1h20m

NUTRITION FACTS

Calories: 705 | Carbohydrates: 37.9g | Fat: 46.8g | Protein: 32.7g | Cholesterol: 123mg

INGREDIENTS

- 1 tablespoon vegetable oil
- 4 potatoes, thinly sliced
- 6 boneless pork chops
- 1/2 cup chopped onion
- 1 (10.75 ounce) can condensed cream of mushroom soup
- 1 cup shredded Cheddar cheese

- 1 cup milk

DIRECTIONS

1. Preheat oven to 400 degrees F (200 degrees C).
2. Heat oil in a large skillet over medium high-heat. Place the pork chops in the oil, and sear.
3. In a medium bowl, combine the soup and the milk. Arrange the potatoes and onions in a 9x13 inch baking dish. Place the browned chops over the potatoes and onions, then pour the soup mixture over all.
4. Bake 30 minutes in the preheated oven. Top with the cheese, and bake for 30 more minutes.

JALAPENO CREAM CHEESE CHICKEN ENCHILADAS

Servings: 7 | Prep: 25m | Cooks: 1h15m | Total: 1h40m

NUTRITION FACTS

Calories: 583 | Carbohydrates: 38.4g | Fat: 35.5g | Protein: 28.7g | Cholesterol: 123mg

INGREDIENTS

- 3 skinless, boneless chicken breast halves
- 1 tablespoon garlic powder
- 1 teaspoon cayenne pepper
- 1/2 teaspoon cayenne pepper
- 1/2 teaspoon garlic powder
- 1/2 teaspoon paprika
- salt and ground black pepper to taste
- 1/2 teaspoon chili powder
- 2 tablespoons butter
- 1/2 teaspoon ground cumin
- 1 large onion, minced
- 1 (28 ounce) can green enchilada sauce
- 2 jalapeno peppers, seeded and minced (wear gloves)
- 7 flour tortillas
- 1 (8 ounce) package cream cheese
- 8 ounces shredded Monterey Jack cheese, divided

DIRECTIONS

1. Preheat oven to 350 degrees F (175 degrees C).
2. Season chicken breasts with 1 teaspoon of cayenne pepper, 1/2 teaspoon of garlic powder, salt, and black pepper. Place into a baking dish.
3. Bake in the preheated oven until the chicken is no longer pink inside and the juices run clear, about 45 minutes. Allow chicken to cool, and shred with 2 forks. Set chicken aside.

4. Heat butter in a large nonstick skillet over medium heat, and cook the onion and jalapenos until the onion is translucent, about 5 minutes; stir in the cream cheese in chunks, and allow cream cheese to melt and soften. Stir in cream cheese, garlic powder, cayenne pepper, paprika, chili powder, and cumin. Mix in the cooked chicken meat; remove from heat.

5. Pour half the green enchilada sauce into the bottom of a 9x13-inch baking dish. Lay tortillas out onto a work surface, and place chicken mixture in a line down the center of each tortilla; sprinkle with about 1 tablespoon of Monterey Jack cheese per tortilla. Roll up the tortillas, and place into the sauce in the dish, seam sides down; pour the remaining sauce over the enchiladas. Sprinkle remaining 4 ounces of Monterey Jack cheese over the top.

6. Bake in the preheated oven until the filling is hot and bubbling and the cheese has melted, 30 to 35 minutes.

CHILI DOG CASSEROLE

Servings: 7 | Prep: 15m | Cooks: 30m | Total: 45m

NUTRITION FACTS

Calories: 608 | Carbohydrates: 33.7g | Fat: 41.4g | Protein: 26.2g | Cholesterol: 94mg

INGREDIENTS

- 8 hot dog buns
- 1/4 cup chopped onion
- 8 hot dogs
- 1 tablespoon prepared mustard
- 1 (15 ounce) can chili
- 2 cups shredded Cheddar cheese

DIRECTIONS

1. Preheat oven to 350 degrees F (175 degrees C).
2. Lightly grease a 9x13 inch baking dish. Tear up the hot dog buns and arrange the pieces in the bottom of the dish evenly. Slice the hot dogs into bite size pieces and layer the pieces over the buns.
3. Pour the chili over the hot dogs, sprinkle with the chopped onion, then spread some mustard over the chili and the onion. Top off with the cheese.
4. Bake at 350 degrees F (175 degrees C) for 30 minutes.

TUNA NOODLE CASSEROLE

Servings: 6 | Prep: 10m | Cooks: 50m | Total: 1h

NUTRITION FACTS

Calories: 346 | Carbohydrates: 34.2g | Fat: 14.6g | Protein: 19.3g | Cholesterol: 71mg

INGREDIENTS

- 1 (8 ounce) package wide egg noodles
- 1 cup milk
- 2 tablespoons butter
- 1 cup shredded sharp Cheddar cheese
- 2 tablespoons all-purpose flour
- 1 (5 ounce) can tuna, drained
- 1 teaspoon salt (optional)
- 1 (15 ounce) can peas, drained

DIRECTIONS

1. Preheat oven to 350 degrees F (175 degrees C). Coat a 2 quart casserole dish with cooking spray.
2. In a large pot of salted water, boil noodles until al dente. Drain well.
3. In a medium saucepan, combine flour, butter, and salt. Stir until butter is melted and ingredients are combined evenly. Add milk, and whisk until the sauce thickens (usually it is at the proper consistency by the time it begins to boil). Add cheese to mixture, and whisk until cheese is melted and mixture is well blended. Stir in tuna, peas, and noodles. Spread evenly in prepared dish.
4. Bake in preheated oven for 30 minutes.

BEEF AND BISCUIT

Servings: 10 | Prep: 20m | Cooks: 25m | Total: 45m

NUTRITION FACTS

Calories: 306 | Carbohydrates: 15.5g | Fat: 18.9g | Protein: 18.4g | Cholesterol: 76mg

INGREDIENTS

- 1 1/4 pounds lean ground beef
- 1/2 teaspoon garlic salt
- 1/2 cup chopped onion
- 1 (10 ounce) can refrigerated buttermilk biscuit dough
- 1/4 cup chopped green chile pepper
- 1 1/2 cups shredded Monterey Jack cheese, divided
- 1 (8 ounce) can tomato sauce
- 1/2 cup sour cream
- 2 teaspoons chili powder
- 1 egg, lightly beaten

DIRECTIONS

1. Preheat oven to 375 degrees F (190 degrees C).

2. In a large skillet, brown the ground beef, onion and green chile pepper; drain. Stir in tomato sauce, chili powder ,and garlic salt. Simmer while preparing the biscuits.

3. Separate biscuit dough into 10 biscuits. Pull each biscuit into 2 layers. Press 10 biscuit halves on the bottom of a 9-inch pie dish to form bottom crust. Reserve the other 10 biscuit halves for the top layer.

4. Remove meat mixture from heat, and stir in 1/2 cup shredded cheese, sour cream, and egg; mix well. Spoon over bottom crust. Arrange remaining biscuit halves to form top crust, and spoon remaining cheese evenly over the top.

5. Bake in preheated oven for 25 to 30 minutes, or until biscuits are a deep golden brown color.

CHERYL'S SPINACH CHEESY PASTA CASSEROLE

Servings: 12 | Prep: 15m | Cooks: 1h | Total: 1h15m

NUTRITION FACTS

Calories: 378 | Carbohydrates: 38g | Fat: 18g | Protein: 17g | Cholesterol: 64mg

INGREDIENTS

- 1 (12 ounce) package medium seashell pasta
- 1/2 cup bread crumbs
- 1 (10 ounce) package frozen chopped spinach, thawed
- 1 1/2 (26 ounce) jars tomato basil pasta sauce
- 2 eggs
- 1 (8 ounce) package shredded Cheddar cheese
- 1/4 cup olive oil
- 1 (8 ounce) package shredded mozzarella cheese

DIRECTIONS

1. Preheat oven to 350 degrees F (175 degrees C).

2. Bring a large pot of lightly salted water to a boil. Cook pasta in boiling water for 8 to 10 minutes, or until al dente; drain. Bring 1/2 cup water to a boil in a saucepan, and cook the spinach 4 to 6 minutes, until tender.

3. Place the cooked pasta in a medium bowl. In a small bowl, whisk together the eggs and oil. Toss the pasta with the cooked spinach, egg mixture, and bread crumbs.

4. Cover the bottom of a 9x13 inch baking dish with 1/3 of the pasta sauce. Pour half of the pasta mixture into the baking dish, and cover with another 1/3 of the pasta sauce. Sprinkle with half of the Cheddar cheese and half of the mozzarella. Layer with remaining pasta mixture, and top with remaining sauce. Sprinkle with the rest of the Cheddar and mozzarella cheeses.

5. Bake 45 minutes in the preheated oven, or until bubbly and lightly browned.

BARBEQUE BEEF CASSEROLE
Servings: 12 | Prep: 15m | Cooks: 25m | Total: 40m

NUTRITION FACTS

Calories: 420 | Carbohydrates: 52.2g | Fat: 15g | Protein: 18.7g | Cholesterol: 48mg

INGREDIENTS

- 2 pounds ground beef
- 1/2 cup barbeque sauce
- 1 large onion, diced
- 1 (14.5 ounce) can diced tomatoes, drained
- 1 green bell pepper, seeded and diced
- 3 (8.5 ounce) packages corn bread mix
- 1 (10 ounce) can whole kernel corn, drained

DIRECTIONS

1. Preheat the oven to 400 degrees F (200 degrees C).
2. Crumble the ground beef into a large skillet over medium-high heat. Cook until evenly browned. Add the onion, bell pepper, corn and tomatoes. Cook and stir until vegetables are tender. Drain excess grease, and stir in the barbeque sauce. Spread the beef mixture in an even layer in a 9x13 inch baking dish.
3. Prepare the cornbread batter mixes according to package directions. Spread the batter over the top of the beef mixture.
4. Bake for 20 to 25 minutes in the preheated oven, until the top is golden brown, and a knife inserted into the center of the cornbread layer comes out clean.

TATER TOT CASSEROLE
Servings: 6 | Prep: 10m | Cooks: 1h | Total: 1h10m

NUTRITION FACTS

Calories: 718 | Carbohydrates: 56.2g | Fat: 53.3g | Protein: 11.5g | Cholesterol: 53mg

INGREDIENTS

- 1 (32 ounce) package frozen potato rounds
- 1 (10.75 ounce) can condensed cream of mushroom soup
- 1 (16 ounce) container sour cream
- 1 (6 ounce) can French-fried onions
- 1 cup shredded Cheddar cheese

DIRECTIONS

1. Preheat oven to 350 degrees F (175 degrees C). Grease a 9x13 inch baking dish.
2. Arrange tater tots in the prepared baking dish.
3. In a mixing bowl, combine sour cream, cheese, and mushroom soup. Pour this mixture over the tater tots. Sprinkle onions over the top of the casserole.
4. Bake in the 350 degrees F (175 degrees C) oven for 45 to 60 minutes.

AMISH YUMAZUTI

Servings: 6 | Prep: 30m | Cooks: 1h | Total: 1h30m

NUTRITION FACTS

Calories: 422 | Carbohydrates: 45.9g | Fat: 16.5g | Protein: g | Cholesterol: 96mg

INGREDIENTS

- 1 pound ground beef
- 1/4 cup shredded Cheddar cheese
- 1 onion, chopped
- 1 (14.5 ounce) can stewed, diced tomatoes
- 3/4 cup chopped celery
- 1 (12 ounce) package uncooked egg noodles
- 1 tablespoon minced garlic
- 1 (10.75 ounce) can condensed cream of chicken soup

DIRECTIONS

1. Preheat the oven to 350 degrees F (175 degrees C). Place noodles in a pot of lightly salted boiling water. Cook until al dente, about 8 minutes. Drain and set aside.
2. Cook ground beef, onion, celery and garlic in a skillet over medium heat until meat is evenly browned. Drain off excess grease.
3. Butter a 9x13 inch baking dish. Place half of the cooked noodles in the bottom of the dish. Cover them with half of the meat mixture, then half of the tomatoes. Spoon half of the cream of chicken soup over the tomatoes, then sprinkle half of the shredded cheese. Repeat layers, ending with cheese on the top.
4. Bake for 1 hour in the preheated oven, or until cheese is browned and bubbly. Let stand for 10 minutes to set before serving.

REUBEN CASSEROLE

Servings: 6 | Prep: 15m | Cooks: 30m | Total: 45m

NUTRITION FACTS

Calories: 450 | Carbohydrates: 30.8g | Fat: 24.3g | Protein: 28.2g | Cholesterol: 82mg

INGREDIENTS

- 6 slices rye bread, cubed
- 3/4 cup Russian-style salad dressing
- 1 (16 ounce) can sauerkraut, drained and rinsed
- 2 cups shredded Swiss cheese
- 1 pound deli sliced corned beef, cut into strips

DIRECTIONS

1. Preheat oven to 400 degrees F (200 degrees C).
2. Spread bread cubes in the bottom of a 9x13 inch baking dish. Spread sauerkraut evenly over the bread cubes, then layer beef strips over sauerkraut. Pour dressing over all.
3. Spray aluminum foil with cooking spray and use to cover baking dish, sprayed side down. Bake in the preheated oven for 20 minutes.
4. Remove cover, sprinkle with cheese and bake uncovered for another 10 minutes, or until cheese is melted and bubbly.

BEST BEEF ENCHILADAS

Servings: 8 | Prep: 25m | Cooks: 20m | Total: 45m

NUTRITION FACTS

Calories: 283 | Carbohydrates: 46.1g | Fat: 29.2g | Protein: 33g | Cholesterol: 94mg

INGREDIENTS

- 2 pounds ground beef
- 2 1/2 cups enchilada sauce
- 1/4 onion, finely chopped
- 1 1/2 teaspoons chili powder
- 1 cup shredded Cheddar cheese
- 1 clove garlic, minced
- 1/2 cup sour cream
- 1/2 teaspoon salt
- 1 tablespoon dried parsley
- 8 flour tortillas
- 1 tablespoon taco seasoning
- 1 (15 ounce) can black beans, rinsed and drained
- 1 teaspoon dried oregano
- 1 (4 ounce) can sliced black olives, drained
- 1/2 teaspoon ground black pepper

* 1/4 cup shredded Cheddar cheese

DIRECTIONS

1. Preheat oven to 350 degrees F (175 degrees C).
2. Cook and stir ground beef with onion in a skillet over medium heat until meat is crumbly and no longer pink, about 10 minutes. Drain grease. Stir 1 cup Cheddar cheese, sour cream, parsley, taco seasoning, oregano, and black pepper into the ground beef until cheese has melted. Mix in enchilada sauce, chili powder, garlic, and salt; bring to a simmer, reduce heat to low, and simmer until meat sauce is slightly thickened, about 5 minutes.
3. Lay a tortilla onto a work surface and spoon about 1/4 cup of meat sauce down the center of the tortilla. Top meat sauce with 1 tablespoon black beans and a sprinkling of black olives. Roll the tortilla up, enclosing the filling, and lay seam-side down into a 9x13-inch baking dish. Repeat with remaining tortillas. Spoon any remaining meat sauce over the enchiladas and scatter any remaining black beans and black olives over the top. Sprinkle tortillas with 1/4 cup Cheddar cheese.
4. Bake in the preheated oven until cheese topping is melted and enchiladas and sauce are bubbling, 20 to 22 minutes. Let stand 5 minutes before serving.

HAMBURGER CASSEROLE

Servings: 6 | Prep: 20m | Cooks: 20m | Total: 40m

NUTRITION FACTS

Calories: 457 | Carbohydrates: 56.1g | Fat: 15.3g | Protein: 24.7g | Cholesterol: 91mg

INGREDIENTS

* 1 pound ground beef
* 1 (14.5 ounce) can peeled and diced tomatoes
* 1 onion, chopped
* 1 (15 ounce) can whole kernel corn, drained
* 1 stalk celery, chopped
* 1/4 cup taco sauce
* 8 ounces egg noodles
* 1 (1 ounce) package taco seasoning mix
* 1 (15 ounce) can chili

DIRECTIONS

1. Preheat oven to 250 degrees F (120 degrees C).
2. In a large skillet over medium heat, combine the ground beef, onion and celery and saute for 10 minutes, or until the meat is browned and the onion is tender. Drain the fat and set aside.

3. In a separate saucepan, cook noodles according to package directions. When cooked, drain the water and stir in the meat mixture, chili, tomatoes, corn, taco sauce, and taco seasoning mix. Mix well and place entire mixture into a 10x15-inch baking dish.
4. Bake in the preheated oven until thoroughly heated and bubbling, about 20 minutes.

KING RANCH CHICKEN CASSEROLE
Servings: 8 | Prep: 30m | Cooks: 45m | Total: 1h15m

NUTRITION FACTS

Calories: 479 | Carbohydrates: 24.9g | Fat: 28g | Protein: 32g | Cholesterol: 100mg

INGREDIENTS

- 1 tablespoon vegetable oil
- 2 tablespoons sour cream
- 1 white onion, diced
- 2 teaspoons ground cumin
- 1 red bell pepper, diced
- 1 teaspoon ancho chile powder
- 1 green bell pepper, diced
- 1/2 teaspoon dried oregano
- 1 (10.75 ounce) can condensed cream of mushroom soup
- 1/4 teaspoon chipotle chile powder
- 1 (10.75 ounce) can condensed cream of chicken soup
- 1 cooked chicken, torn into shreds or cut into chunks
- 1 (10 ounce) can diced tomatoes with green chile peppers (such as RO*TEL®)
- 8 ounces shredded Cheddar cheese
- 1 cup chicken broth
- 10 corn tortillas, cut into quarters

DIRECTIONS

1. Preheat oven to 350 degrees F (175 degrees C).
2. Heat oil in a large skillet over high heat. Saute onion, red bell pepper, and green bell pepper in hot oil until warmed through, about 2 minutes.
3. Combine onion-pepper mixture, cream of mushroom soup, cream of chicken soup, diced tomatoes, chicken broth, sour cream, cumin, ancho chile powder, oregano, and chipotle chile powder together in a large bowl and stir until sauce is well-combined.
4. Spread a few tablespoons of the sauce in the bottom of a 9x13-inch baking dish. Spread 1/2 the chicken over the sauce. Spread about half the sauce over the chicken and top with 1/3 the cheese. Spread a layer of tortillas over the cheese. Spread remaining 1/2 the chicken over the tortillas, and top with almost all of the remaining sauce, reserving 1/2 cup sauce. Top with 1/3 the cheese, remaining tortillas, the reserved 1/2 cup sauce, and remaining 1/3 cheese.

5. Bake casserole in the preheated oven until bubbling, about 40 minutes. Increase the oven temperature to broil. Broil the casserole until top is golden, 2 to 3 minutes more.

CHICKEN ENCHILADAS WITH CREAMY GREEN CHILE SAUCE

Servings: 6 | Prep: 30m | Cooks: 30m | Total: 1h

NUTRITION FACTS

Calories: 798 | Carbohydrates: 33.3g | Fat: 51.9g | Protein: 49.8g | Cholesterol: 172mg

INGREDIENTS

- 12 corn tortillas
- 1/4 cup all-purpose flour
- vegetable oil for pan-frying
- 2 cups chicken broth
- 3 cooked boneless skinless chicken breast halves, shredded
- 1 cup sour cream
- 12 ounces shredded Monterey Jack cheese, divided
- 1 (4 ounce) can chopped green chiles, drained
- 3/4 cup minced onion
- 1/2 cup chopped green onions
- 1/4 cup butter
- 1/2 cup chopped fresh cilantro

DIRECTIONS

1. Preheat oven to 375 degrees F (190 degrees C). Grease a 9x13-inch baking dish.
2. Heat 2 tablespoons of oil in a skillet over medium-high heat. Fry tortillas (1 at a time) for 5 seconds on each side to soften and make them pliable. Add more oil to pan as needed. Drain between layers of paper towel and keep warm.
3. Divide chicken, 10 ounces of Monterey Jack cheese, and onion among the 12 tortillas. Roll up each tortilla and place seam-side down in the prepared pan.
4. Melt butter in a saucepan over medium heat. Add flour and whisk until mixture begins to boil. Slowly add broth, stirring with a whisk until thickened. Mix in the sour cream and chiles, heating thoroughly but do not boil, stirring occasionally. Pour mixture over the enchiladas.
5. Bake in the preheated oven until bubbly and heated through, about 20 minutes. Top with remaining Monterey Jack cheese and bake for 5 more minutes. Garnish with chopped green onions and cilantro.

SANDY'S CASSEROLE

Servings: 6 | Prep: 5m | Cooks: 45m | Total: 50m

NUTRITION FACTS

Calories: 508 | Carbohydrates: 40.2g | Fat: 24.6g | Protein: 30.3g | Cholesterol: 84mg

INGREDIENTS

- 2 cups uncooked elbow macaroni
- 2 (10.75 ounce) cans condensed cream of chicken soup
- 2 (5 ounce) cans chunk chicken
- 1 (4 ounce) can sliced mushrooms
- 2 cups shredded Cheddar cheese
- 1/4 cup chopped onion
- 2 cups milk

DIRECTIONS

1. Preheat oven to 350 degrees F (175 degrees C).
2. In a large bowl combine the macaroni, chicken, cheese, milk, soup, mushrooms and onion. Mix together and transfer mixture to a 9x13 inch baking dish.
3. Bake at 350 degrees F (175 degrees C) for about 45 minutes, or until bubbly and golden brown.

TATER TOT CASSEROLE

Servings: 10 | Prep: 20m | Cooks: 35m | Total: 55m

NUTRITION FACTS

Calories: 475 | Carbohydrates: 25.8g | Fat: 36.4g | Protein: 16g | Cholesterol: 96mg

INGREDIENTS

- 1 pound ground pork breakfast sausage
- 2 eggs
- 2 cups shredded Cheddar cheese
- 2 pounds tater tots
- 2 cups milk

DIRECTIONS

1. Preheat oven to 350 degrees F (175 degrees C).
2. Place sausage in a large, deep skillet. Cook over medium-high heat until evenly brown. Drain, and spread evenly in the bottom of a 9x13 inch pan. Spread cheese over sausage.

3. In large bowl, beat together milk and eggs. Pour over cheese. (May be refrigerated overnight at this point).Top with tater tots.
4. Bake in preheated oven for 35 to 45 minutes. Cool for 5 to 10 minutes before serving.

CHICKEN OR TURKEY TETRAZZINI DELUXE
Servings: 12 | Prep: 25m | Cooks: 35m | Total: 1h

NUTRITION FACTS

Calories: 493 | Carbohydrates: 39g | Fat: 24.7g | Protein: 28.8g | Cholesterol: 85mg

INGREDIENTS

- 1 (16 ounce) package linguine pasta
- 1 (10 ounce) package frozen green peas
- 1/2 cup butter
- 1/2 cup cooking sherry
- 3 cups sliced fresh mushrooms
- 1 teaspoon Worcestershire sauce
- 1 cup minced onion
- 1 teaspoon salt
- 1 cup minced green bell pepper
- 1/4 teaspoon ground black pepper
- 2 (10.75 ounce) cans condensed cream of mushroom soup
- 4 cups chopped cooked chicken breast
- 2 cups chicken broth
- 1 cup grated Parmesan cheese
- 2 cups shredded sharp Cheddar cheese
- paprika to taste

DIRECTIONS

1. Bring a large pot of lightly salted water to a boil. Add pasta and cook for 8 to 10 minutes or until al dente; drain and set aside.
2. Preheat oven to 375 degrees F (190 degrees C).
3. Meanwhile, melt butter in a large saucepan over medium heat. Add mushrooms, onion and bell pepper and saute until tender. Stir in cream of mushroom soup and chicken broth; cook, stirring, until heated through. Stir in pasta, Cheddar cheese, peas, sherry, Worcestershire sauce, salt, pepper and chicken. Mix well and transfer mixture to a lightly greased 11x14 inch baking dish. Sprinkle with Parmesan cheese and paprika.
4. Bake in the preheated oven for 25 to 35 minutes, or until heated through.

CHEESE'S BAKED MACARONI AND CHEESE

Servings: 8 | Prep: 20m | Cooks: 45m | Total: 1h20m | Additional: 15m

NUTRITION FACTS

Calories: 600 | Carbohydrates: 39.2g | Fat: 38.3g | Protein: 24.1g | Cholesterol: 101mg

INGREDIENTS

- 1 (16 ounce) package fully cooked kielbasa sausage, cut into 1/2-inch pieces
- 2 cups milk
- 1 (8 ounce) package elbow macaroni
- 1 (10 ounce) package sharp Cheddar cheese, cubed
- 1/3 cup butter
- salt and ground black pepper to taste
- 1 small onion, chopped
- 1 cup dry bread crumbs, or more as needed
- 3 tablespoons all-purpose flour

DIRECTIONS

1. Cook and stir the cut-up kielbasa in a large skillet over medium heat for 6 to 8 minutes, until heated through and beginning to brown. Remove the sausage from the skillet, and set aside.
2. Fill a pan with lightly salted water, bring to a boil over medium-high heat, stir in the macaroni, and return to a boil. Cook, stirring occasionally, until the pasta has cooked through but is still firm to the bite, about 8 minutes. Drain well.
3. Preheat an oven to 350 degrees F (175 degrees C). Grease a 9x13 inch baking dish.
4. Melt the butter in the skillet over medium-low heat, and cook and stir the chopped onion for about 5 minutes, until translucent. Whisk in the flour, stirring constantly to avoid lumps. Cook and stir the butter, onion and flour for 2 to 3 minutes to make a roux, and remove from the heat. Whisk in the milk a little at a time, stirring constantly, until all the milk has been incorporated, and return to low heat. Bring the sauce to a simmer, and cook over low heat for about 2 minutes, stirring constantly, to finish cooking the flour. Whisk in the Cheddar cheese, a few cubes at a time, until all the cheese has been incorporated and the sauce is hot and smooth.
5. Pour the macaroni into the cheese sauce, and stir to combine. Stir in the cooked kielbasa, salt, and pepper.
6. Spoon the macaroni mixture into the prepared baking dish, and sprinkle the bread crumbs over the top. Bake for about 20 minutes in the preheated oven, until the crumbs are brown and the casserole is bubbling. Let stand for 15 minutes after baking, to set before serving.

CALICO BEAN CASSEROLE

Servings: 6 | Prep: 20m | Cooks: 30m | Total: 50m

Calories: 617 | Carbohydrates: 69.2g | Fat: 26.1g | Protein: 27.6g | Cholesterol: 75mg

INGREDIENTS

- 1 (15 ounce) can kidney beans, undrained
- 3/4 cup packed brown sugar
- 1 (16 ounce) can baked beans with pork
- 1 pound lean ground beef
- 1 (15 ounce) can butter beans, undrained
- 4 ounces bacon, chopped
- 1/2 cup ketchup
- 1/2 cup chopped onion
- 2 teaspoons white vinegar
- salt to taste
- 1 tablespoon dry mustard
- ground black pepper to taste

DIRECTIONS

1. Preheat oven to 350 degrees F (175 degrees C).
2. In a large skillet over medium heat, fry the ground beef, bacon and onion together until ground beef is no longer pink. Drain fat.
3. In a large mixing bowl, combine the kidney beans, baked beans with pork and butter beans. Stir in the ketchup, white vinegar, dry mustard, brown sugar and cook beef mixture. Mix thoroughly, adding salt and pepper to taste.
4. Pour the bean and meat mixture into a 9x13 inch baking dish. Bake in preheated oven for 30 to 40 minutes.

MEXICAN QUESADILLA CASSEROLE

Servings: 8 | Prep: 15m | Cooks: 25m | Total: 45m | Additional: 5m

NUTRITION FACTS

Calories: 493 | Carbohydrates: 50.1g | Fat: 21.2g | Protein: 26.6g | Cholesterol: 65mg

INGREDIENTS

- cooking spray
- 2 teaspoons chili powder
- 1 pound ground beef
- 1 teaspoon ground cumin
- 1/2 cup chopped onion

- 1 teaspoon minced garlic
- 1 (15 ounce) can tomato sauce
- 1/2 teaspoon dried oregano
- 1 (15 ounce) can black beans, rinsed and drained
- 1/2 teaspoon red pepper flakes
- 1 (14.5 ounce) can diced tomatoes with lime juice and cilantro (such as RO*TEL®)
- 6 flour tortillas
- 1 (8.75 ounce) can whole kernel sweet corn, drained
- 2 cups shredded Cheddar cheese
- 1 (4.5 ounce) can chopped green chiles, drained

DIRECTIONS

1. Preheat oven to 350 degrees F (175 degrees C). Prepare a 13x9-inch baking dish with cooking spray.
2. Heat a large skillet over medium-high heat. Cook and stir beef and onion in the hot skillet until beef is completely browned, 5 to 7 minutes; drain and discard grease.
3. Stir tomato sauce, black beans, diced tomatoes with lime juice and cilantro, corn, and chopped green chiles into the ground beef mixture; season with chili powder, cumin, garlic, oregano, and red pepper flakes. Reduce heat to low and cook mixture at a simmer for 5 minutes.
4. Spread about 1/2 cup beef mixture into the bottom of the prepared baking dish; top with 3 tortillas, overlapping as needed. Spread another 1/2 cup beef mixture over the tortillas. Sprinkle 1 cup Cheddar cheese over beef. Finish with layers of remaining tortillas, beef mixture, and Cheddar cheese, respectively.
5. Bake in preheated oven until heated throughout and the cheese is melted, about 15 minutes. Cool 5 minutes before serving.

DEB'S SCALLOPS FLORENTINE
Servings: 6 | Prep: 30m | Cooks: 25m | Total: 55m

NUTRITION FACTS

Calories: 376 | Carbohydrates: 11.5g | Fat: 26.6g | Protein: 23.4g | Cholesterol: 112mg

INGREDIENTS

- 1 pound sea scallops
- ground black pepper to taste
- 3 tablespoons butter
- 1 (10 ounce) package frozen chopped spinach, thawed
- 2 tablespoons all-purpose flour
- 1 cup shredded mozzarella cheese
- 1 cup heavy cream
- 1/4 cup grated Parmesan cheese

- 1/4 cup grated Parmesan cheese
- 1/4 cup plain bread crumbs
- salt to taste
- 1 tablespoon OLD BAY® Seasoning

DIRECTIONS

1. Preheat oven to 350 degrees F (175 degrees C). Lightly grease a 9 inch pie plate.
2. Bring a pot of water to a rolling boil. Rinse the scallops, and drop them into the boiling water; cook for 2 minutes. Remove the scallops with a slotted spoon, and pat dry. Place on the bottom of the prepared pie plate.
3. In a small saucepan, melt the butter, and stir in the flour. Cook over low heat for 3 minutes. Whisk in heavy cream and 1/4 cup Parmesan cheese. Season with salt and pepper to taste. Cook for another 2 to 3 minutes, stirring constantly, or until thick.
4. Squeeze the spinach dry, and spread over the scallops. Pour the cream sauce over the spinach, and top with mozzarella cheese, 1/4 cup Parmesan cheese, and bread crumbs. Sprinkle Old Bay Seasoning over the bread crumbs.
5. Bake in preheated oven for 15 minutes, or until browned and bubbly.

GRANDMA'S GROUND BEEF CASSEROLE
Servings: 6 | Prep: 20m | Cooks: 55m | Total: 1h15m

NUTRITION FACTS

Calories: 519 | Carbohydrates: 39.4g | Fat: 29.8g | Protein: 24.5g | Cholesterol: 120mg

INGREDIENTS

- 1 pound ground beef
- 1 (8 ounce) package egg noodles
- 1 teaspoon white sugar
- 1 cup sour cream
- 1 teaspoon salt
- 1 (3 ounce) package cream cheese
- 1 teaspoon garlic salt
- 1 large white onion, diced
- 2 (15 ounce) cans tomato sauce
- 1/2 cup shredded sharp Cheddar cheese, or more to taste

DIRECTIONS

1. Heat a large skillet over medium-high heat. Cook and stir beef in the hot skillet until browned and crumbly, 5 to 7 minutes; drain and discard grease. Mix sugar, salt, garlic salt and tomato sauce into

ground beef; simmer until flavors blend, about 20 minutes. Remove from heat, cover skillet, and cool to room temperature.

2. Bring a large pot of lightly salted water to a boil. Cook egg noodles in the boiling water, stirring occasionally until cooked through but firm to the bite, about 5 minutes. Drain and cool slightly.

3. Preheat oven to 350 degrees F (175 degrees C). Grease a 9x13-inch casserole dish.

4. Mix sour cream, cream cheese, and onion in a bowl.

5. Scoop half the noodles into the prepared casserole dish; top with half the sour cream mixture. Spoon half the ground beef mixture atop sour cream layer. Repeat layering with remaining ingredients. Top casserole with Cheddar cheese.

6. Bake in the preheated oven until Cheddar cheese has browned, 25 to 30 minutes.

PORK CHOPS AND SCALLOPED POTATOES

Servings: 6 | Prep: 30m | Cooks: 1h30m | Total: 2h

NUTRITION FACTS

Calories: 300 | Carbohydrates: 29.6g | Fat: 12.4g | Protein: 17.6g | Cholesterol: 54mg

INGREDIENTS

- 3 tablespoons butter, divided
- 1 (14.5 ounce) can chicken broth
- 1 1/2 teaspoons salt
- 6 pork chops
- 1/4 teaspoon ground black pepper
- 6 cups thinly sliced potatoes
- 3 tablespoons all-purpose flour
- 1 dash paprika

DIRECTIONS

1. Preheat oven to 350 degrees F (175 degrees C).
2. In sauce pan melt 1 tablespoon butter over medium heat. Add salt, pepper and flour. Pour in the chicken broth, cook and stir until mixture boils. Remove from heat and set aside.
3. In skillet brown pork chops in 1 tablespoon butter. Grease a cooking dish with the remaining tablespoon butter and layer potatoes. Pour mixture over potatoes and place browned chops on top. Sprinkle paprika on top.
4. Cover and bake for 1 hour. Uncover and bake for an additional 30 minutes.

PORK CHOPS AND SCALLOPED POTATOES

Servings: 8 | Prep: 30m | Cooks: 1h | Total: 1h30m

NUTRITION FACTS

Calories: 375 | Carbohydrates: 28g | Fat: 17.1g | Protein: 27.9g | Cholesterol: 77mg

INGREDIENTS

- 1 (10.75 ounce) can condensed cream of chicken soup
- 1 onion, chopped
- 1 (10.75 ounce) can condensed cream of mushroom soup
- 1 green bell pepper, chopped
- 2 cups chicken broth
- 8 ounces shredded Cheddar cheese
- 1 (10 ounce) can diced tomatoes with green chile peppers
- 1 1/2 teaspoons chili powder
- 1 (12 ounce) package corn tortillas
- 1 teaspoon garlic salt
- 3 cups cooked, diced chicken breast meat

DIRECTIONS

1. Preheat oven to 350 degrees F (175 degrees C).
2. Combine the chicken soup, mushroom soup, broth and tomatoes with chiles. Set aside.
3. Lightly grease a shallow 3 quart casserole dish. Layer 1/2 the tortillas, 1/2 the chicken, 1/2 the onion, 1/2 the bell pepper and 1/2 the cheese in the casserole dish. Pour 1/2 of the soup mixture over the layers. Repeat the layers of tortillas, chicken, onion and bell pepper; pour the remaining soup mixture over the top, then top with the remaining cheese. Sprinkle with chili powder and garlic salt and bake for 30 to 45 minutes.

CHEESEBURGER AND FRIES CASSEROLE

Servings: 8 | Prep: 20m | Cooks: 20m | Total: 40m

NUTRITION FACTS

Calories: 511 | Carbohydrates: 21.1g | Fat: 32g | Protein: 33.7g | Cholesterol: 121mg

INGREDIENTS

- 2 pounds lean ground beef
- 1 (10.75 ounce) can condensed golden mushroom soup
- 1/2 medium onion, chopped
- 1 (10.75 ounce) can condensed Cheddar cheese soup
- salt and pepper to taste
- 1 (16 ounce) package frozen French fries
- garlic powder to taste
- 2 cups shredded Cheddar cheese

DIRECTIONS

1. Preheat the oven to 375 degrees F (190 degrees C).
2. Combine the ground beef and onion in a skillet over medium-high heat. Cook, stirring occasionally until beef is no longer pink, and the onion is translucent. Drain off excess grease, and season with salt, pepper and garlic powder.
3. Return to the heat, and stir in the golden mushroom and cheese soups until well blended. Heat through, and remove from stove. Transfer the mixture to a 9x13 inch baking dish. Cover the ground beef mixture with a layer of frozen French fries.
4. Bake for 25 to 30 minutes in the preheated oven. When the fries are golden brown, remove the casserole from the oven, and sprinkle cheese over the top. Return to the oven, and bake just until cheese has melted.

PIEROGI CASSEROLE

Servings: 8 | Prep: 45m | Cooks: 45m | Total: 1h30m

NUTRITION FACTS

Calories: 626 | Carbohydrates: 48.2g | Fat: 40.7g | Protein: 18.6g | Cholesterol: 93mg

INGREDIENTS

- 5 potatoes, peeled and cubed
- 1/2 (16 ounce) package lasagna noodles
- 1/2 cup milk
- 2 cups shredded Cheddar cheese
- 1/2 cup butter, melted
- salt and pepper to taste
- 1/2 pound bacon, diced
- 1 (8 ounce) container sour cream
- 1 onion, chopped
- 3 tablespoons chopped fresh chives
- 6 cloves garlic, minced

DIRECTIONS

1. Preheat oven to 350 degrees F (175 degrees C).
2. Place the potatoes in a large pot with water to cover over high heat. Bring to a boil and cook until the potatoes are tender. Remove from heat, drain, then combine with the milk and 6 tablespoons of butter, mash and set aside.
3. Melt the remaining 2 tablespoons of the butter in a large skillet over medium high heat. Saute the bacon, onion and garlic in the butter for 5 to 10 minutes, or until the bacon is fully cooked.
4. Cook the lasagna noodles according to package directions and cool under running water.

5. Place 1/2 of the mashed potatoes into the bottom of a 9x13 inch baking dish. Top this with 1/3 of the cheese, followed by a layer of lasagna noodles. Repeat this with the remaining potatoes, another 1/3 of the cheese and a layer of noodles. Then arrange the bacon, onion and garlic over the noodles, then another layer of noodles, and finally top all with the remaining cheese. Season with salt and pepper to taste.

6. Bake, uncovered, at 350 degrees F (175 degrees C) for 30 to 45 minutes, or until the cheese is melted and bubbly. Serve with sour cream and chopped fresh chives.

AUNT JEWEL'S CHICKEN DRESSING CASSEROLE

Servings: 612 | Prep: 15m | Cooks: 45m | Total: 1h

NUTRITION FACTS

Calories: 236 | Carbohydrates: 15.8g | Fat: 5.2g | Protein: 29.5g | Cholesterol: 73mg

INGREDIENTS

- 3 pounds skinless, boneless chicken breast meat
- 1 (10.75 ounce) can milk
- 1 (10.75 ounce) can condensed cream of chicken soup
- 1 1/2 cups chicken broth
- 1 (10.75 ounce) can condensed cream of celery soup
- 1 (6 ounce) package seasoned cornbread stuffing mix

DIRECTIONS

1. Place chicken in a large saucepan full of lightly salted water. Bring to a boil; boil for about 30 minutes, or until chicken is cooked through (juices run clear). Remove chicken from pan, reserving broth. Cut chicken into bite size pieces and place in bottom of a 9x13 inch baking dish.
2. Preheat oven to 350 degrees F (175 degrees C).
3. In a medium bowl mix together cream of chicken soup and cream of celery soup. Fill one empty soup can with milk, and mix milk with soups. Pour mixture over chicken. In a small bowl combine stuffing and broth; mix together and spoon mixture over casserole.
4. Bake in the preheated oven for 45 minutes.

COWBOY CASSEROLE

Servings: 5 | Prep: 5m | Cooks: 20m | Total: 25m

NUTRITION FACTS

Calories: 601 | Carbohydrates: 62g | Fat: 25.2g | Protein: 32.8g | Cholesterol: 84mg

INGREDIENTS

- 1/2 pound bacon
- 2 (15 ounce) cans baked beans with pork
- 1 pound ground beef
- 1/3 cup barbeque sauce
- 1 small onion, chopped
- 1 (7.5 ounce) package refrigerated biscuit dough

DIRECTIONS

1. Cook bacon in a large skillet or Dutch oven over medium heat until evenly browned. Drain, and cut into bite size pieces. Set aside. Add hamburger and onion to the skillet, and cook until no longer pink, and the onion is tender. Drain.
2. Stir bacon, baked beans and barbeque sauce into the ground beef, and bring to a boil. Reduce heat to medium low, and place biscuits in a single layer over the top of the mixture. Cover, and simmer for about 10 minutes, or until the biscuits are done. Place two biscuits on each plate, and spoon beans over.

CHICKEN AND PASTA CASSEROLE WITH MIXED VEGETABLES

Servings: 6 | Prep: 15m | Cooks: 45m | Total: 1h

NUTRITION FACTS

Calories: 395 | Carbohydrates: 35.4g | Fat: 19.8g | Protein: 19.8g | Cholesterol: 47mg

INGREDIENTS

- 1 cup dry fusilli pasta
- 1 tablespoon dried parsley
- 3 tablespoons olive oil
- 1 (10.75 ounce) can condensed cream of chicken soup
- 6 chicken tenderloins, cut into chunks
- 1 (10.75 ounce) can condensed cream of mushroom soup
- 1 tablespoon dried minced onion
- 2 cups frozen mixed vegetables
- salt and pepper to taste
- 1 cup dry bread crumbs
- garlic powder to taste
- 2 tablespoons grated Parmesan cheese
- 1 tablespoon dried basil
- 2 tablespoons butter, melted

DIRECTIONS

1. Preheat oven to 400 degrees F (200 degrees C). Lightly grease a medium baking dish.
2. Bring a large pot of lightly salted water to a boil. Place fusilli pasta in the pot, cook for 8 to 10 minutes, until al dente, and drain.
3. Heat the oil in a skillet over medium heat. Place chicken in the skillet, and season with minced onion, salt and pepper, garlic powder, basil, and parsley. Cook until chicken juices run clear. Mix in the cooked pasta, cream of chicken soup, cream of mushroom soup, and mixed vegetables. Transfer to the prepared baking dish.
4. In a small bowl, mix the bread crumbs, Parmesan cheese, and butter. Spread evenly over the casserole.
5. Bake 30 minutes in the preheated oven until bubbly and lightly browned.

SAUSAGE BRUNCH CASSEROLE

Servings: 12 | Prep: 15m | Cooks: 15m | Total: 30m

NUTRITION FACTS

Calories: 385 | Carbohydrates: 9.3g | Fat: 31.8g | Protein: 15.1g | Cholesterol: 114mg

INGREDIENTS

- 1 1/2 pounds ground pork sausage
- 4 eggs, beaten
- 1 (8 ounce) package refrigerated crescent roll dough
- 3/4 cup milk
- 2 cups mozzarella cheese
- salt and pepper to taste

DIRECTIONS

1. Place sausage in a large, deep skillet. Cook over medium high heat until evenly brown. Drain, crumble and set aside. Preheat oven to 425 degrees F (220 degrees C).
2. Lightly grease a 9x13 inch baking pan. Lay crescent rolls flat in the bottom of the pan. Combine cooked sausage, cheese, eggs, milk, salt and pepper; pour over crescent rolls.
3. Bake in preheated oven for 15 minutes, until bubbly and rolls are baked.

BAKED SEAFOOD AU GRATIN

Servings: 8 | Prep: 20m | Cooks: 1h | Total: 1h20m

NUTRITION FACTS

Calories: 566 | Carbohydrates: 20.4g | Fat: 34.2g | Protein: 42.8g | Cholesterol: 233mg

INGREDIENTS

- 1 onion, chopped
- 1/2 pound flounder fillets
- 1 green bell pepper, chopped
- 3 cups milk
- 1 cup butter, divided
- 1 cup shredded sharp Cheddar cheese
- 1 cup all-purpose flour, divided
- 1 tablespoon distilled white vinegar
- 1 pound fresh crabmeat
- 1 teaspoon Worcestershire sauce
- 4 cups water
- 1/2 teaspoon salt
- 1 pound fresh shrimp, peeled and deveined
- 1 pinch ground black pepper
- 1/2 pound small scallops
- 1 dash hot pepper sauce
- 1/2 cup grated Parmesan cheese

DIRECTIONS

1. In a heavy skillet, saute the onion and the pepper in 1/2 cup of butter. Cook until tender. Mix in 1/2 cup of the flour, and cook over medium heat for 10 minutes, stirring frequently. Stir in crabmeat, remove from heat, and set aside.
2. In a large Dutch oven, bring the water to a boil. Add the shrimp, scallops, and flounder, and simmer for 3 minutes. Drain, reserving 1 cup of the cooking liquid, and set the seafood aside.
3. In a heavy saucepan, melt the remaining 1/2 cup butter over low heat. Stir in remaining 1/2 cup flour. Cook and stir constantly for 1 minute. Gradually add the milk plus the 1 cup reserved cooking liquid. Raise heat to medium; cook, stirring constantly, until the mixture is thickened and bubbly. Mix in the shredded Cheddar cheese, vinegar, Worcestershire sauce, salt, pepper, and hot sauce. Stir in cooked seafood.
4. Preheat oven to 350 degrees F (175 degrees C). Lightly grease one 9x13 inch baking dish. Press crabmeat mixture into the bottom of the prepared pan. Spoon the seafood mixture over the crabmeat crust, and sprinkle with the Parmesan cheese.
5. Bake in the preheated oven for 30 minutes, or until lightly browned. Serve immediately.

HAMBURGER PIE

Servings: 6 | Prep: 15m | Cooks: 45m | Total: 1h

NUTRITION FACTS

Calories: 424 | Carbohydrates: 43.4g | Fat: 18.3g | Protein: 22.6g | Cholesterol: 66mg

INGREDIENTS

- 4 potatoes
- 2 (10.75 ounce) cans condensed tomato soup
- 1 pound lean ground beef
- 1 (15 ounce) can green beans, drained
- 1 onion, chopped
- 1 cup shredded Cheddar cheese

DIRECTIONS

1. Preheat oven to 350 degrees F (175 degrees C).
2. Bring a large pot of salted water to a boil. Peel and quarter potatoes, and introduce into boiling water; cook until tender, about 15 minutes. Drain and mash. Set aside.
3. In a large skillet over medium-high heat, cook ground beef and onion until beef is brown. Drain. Stir in tomato soup and green beans. Pour into a 9x13 baking dish. Mound mashed potatoes in a ring around the meat mixture (do not cover meat). Sprinkle potatoes with shredded cheese.
4. Bake in preheated oven 30 minutes, until potatoes are golden.

HAM CASSEROLE

Servings: 8 | Prep: 20m | Cooks: 50m | Total: 1h155m | Additional: 5m

NUTRITION FACTS

Calories: 304 | Carbohydrates: 16.9g | Fat: 21.1g | Protein: 12g | Cholesterol: 60mg

INGREDIENTS

- 2 cups peeled and cubed potatoes
- 1/4 cup butter
- 2 stalks celery, chopped
- 3 tablespoons all-purpose flour
- 1 large carrot, sliced
- 1 cup milk, or more as needed
- 3 cups water
- 1/8 teaspoon salt
- 3 tablespoons butter
- 1/8 teaspoon ground black pepper
- 2 cups cubed fully cooked ham
- 1 cup shredded Cheddar cheese
- 2 tablespoons chopped green bell pepper
- 1/2 cup dry bread crumbs
- 2 teaspoons chopped onion

DIRECTIONS

1. Preheat oven to 350 degrees F (175 degrees C).
2. Place potatoes, celery, and carrot in a large pot and cover with water; bring to a boil. Reduce heat to medium-low and simmer until tender, about 20 minutes. Drain and transfer to a 2-quart baking dish.
3. Melt 3 tablespoons butter in a large skillet over medium heat; cook and stir ham, green bell pepper, and onion until vegetables are tender, about 5 minutes. Transfer ham mixture to baking dish and mix with potatoes.
4. Melt remaining 1/4 cup butter in a clean skillet; cook and stir flour in melted butter until smooth, about 3 minutes. Gradually stir in milk and season with salt and black pepper. Bring to a boil, stirring constantly, until thickened, about 2 minutes. Add Cheddar cheese; stir until melted. Pour cheese mixture over ham and potatoes. Sprinkle with bread crumbs.
5. Bake in preheated oven until bubbly, 25 to 30 minutes. Allow casserole to rest for 5 to 10 minutes before serving.

SAVORY TATER TOT CASSEROLE

Servings: 7 | Prep: 5m | Cooks: 1h | Total: 1h5m

NUTRITION FACTS

Calories: 573 | Carbohydrates: 47.9g | Fat: 35g | Protein: 24.2g | Cholesterol: 77mg

INGREDIENTS

- 1 1/2 pounds lean ground beef
- 1 (19 ounce) can cream of chicken soup
- 1/2 onion, chopped
- 1 (32 ounce) package frozen potato rounds
- 4 cups frozen mixed vegetables

DIRECTIONS

1. Preheat oven to 375 degrees F (190 degrees C). Spray 9x13 glass baking dish with cooking spray.
2. Spread hamburger into bottom of pan, covering entire bottom, gently tamping beef down. Sprinkle with diced onions. Layer frozen veggies as next layer. Cover with the soup, straight from the can, carefully spreading with spatula to cover entirely.
3. Layer tater tots on top, covering entire top with tots. Bake at 375 degrees F (190 degrees) for 1 hour, or until hamburger is done. Check after 30 minutes; if tots are getting too brown, turn down to 350 degrees F (190 degrees C).

FARMER'S CASSEROLE

Servings: 6 | Prep: 25m | Cooks: 45m | Total: 1h10m

NUTRITION FACTS

Calories: 316 | Carbohydrates: 21.4g | Fat: 22.4g | Protein: 17.8g | Cholesterol: 173mg

INGREDIENTS

- 3 cups frozen hash brown potatoes
- 4 eggs, beaten
- 3/4 cup shredded pepperjack cheese
- 1 (12 fluid ounce) can evaporated milk
- 1 cup cooked ham, diced
- 1/4 teaspoon ground black pepper
- 1/4 cup chopped green onions
- 1/8 teaspoon salt

DIRECTIONS

1. Preheat oven to 350 degrees F (175 degrees C). Grease a 2 quart baking dish.
2. Arrange hash brown potatoes evenly in the bottom of the prepared dish. Sprinkle with pepperjack cheese, ham, and green onions.
3. In a medium bowl, mix the eggs, evaporated milk, pepper, and salt. Pour the egg mixture over the potato mixture in the dish. The dish may be covered and refrigerated at this point for several hours or overnight.
4. Bake for 40 to 45 minutes (or 55 to 60 minutes if made ahead and chilled) in the preheated oven, or until a knife inserted in the center comes out clean. Let stand 5 minutes before serving.

HAM AND NOODLE CASSEROLE

Servings: 6 | Prep: 20m | Cooks: 50m | Total: 1h10m

NUTRITION FACTS

Calories: 464 | Carbohydrates: 31.2g | Fat: 26.7g | Protein: 24.4g | Cholesterol: 92mg

INGREDIENTS

- 6 cups water
- 2 cups diced cooked ham
- 4 cups uncooked egg noodles
- 2 cups shredded Swiss cheese
- 1 onion, chopped
- salt and pepper to taste
- 1/2 cup sour cream
- 1/4 cup dry bread crumbs
- 1 (10.75 ounce) can condensed cream of chicken soup

DIRECTIONS

1. Preheat an oven to 350 degrees F (175 degrees C). Grease a 2-quart casserole.
2. Bring water to a full rolling boil in a pot.. Cook the egg noodles in the boiling water, stirring occasionally, for 3 minutes; remove from heat, cover, and let stand until the noodles are tender, about 10 minutes. Drain.
3. Stir the noodles, onion, sour cream, chicken soup, ham, and Swiss cheese together in a large bowl. Season with salt and pepper. Spoon into the prepared casserole. Sprinkle the top with bread crumbs.
4. Bake in the preheated oven until the casserole is bubbling and the bread crumbs have browned, about 40 minutes.

BUFFALO CHICKEN AND ROASTED POTATO CASSEROLE

Servings: 10 | Prep: 20m | Cooks: 1h | Total: 1h20m

NUTRITION FACTS

Calories: 501 | Carbohydrates: 33.8g | Fat: 25.5g | Protein: 34.4g | Cholesterol: 92mg

INGREDIENTS

- cooking spray
- 1 1/2 teaspoons salt
- 6 tablespoons hot pepper sauce
- 8 potatoes, cut into 1/2-inch cubes
- 1/3 cup olive oil
- 2 pounds skinless, boneless chicken breast halves, cut into 1/2-inch cubes
- 2 tablespoons garlic powder
- 2 cups shredded Mexican cheese blend (such as Great Value Fiesta Blend®)
- 1 tablespoon freshly ground black pepper
- 1 cup crumbled cooked bacon
- 1 tablespoon paprika
- 1 cup diced green onions

DIRECTIONS

1. Preheat oven to 500 degrees F (260 degrees C). Spray a 9x13-inch baking dish with cooking spray.
2. Heat hot pepper sauce, olive oil, garlic powder, black pepper, paprika, and salt in a large skillet over low heat, stirring until thoroughly combined. Turn off heat. Toss potatoes in batches with the hot pepper sauce mixture to coat and use a slotted spoon to transfer potatoes to the prepared baking dish. Leave remaining sauce in skillet. Mix chicken into remaining sauce and allow to marinate while potatoes roast.
3. Bake potatoes until tender inside and crisp and brown outside, 45 to 50 minutes, stirring every 10 to 15 minutes
4. Reduce oven heat to 400 degrees F (205 degrees C).

5. Spread chicken cubes over roasted potatoes. Sprinkle Mexican cheese blend, cooked bacon, and green onions over chicken. Return to oven and bake until chicken is cooked through and the cheese topping is bubbling, about 15 minutes.

6. Bake in oven until chicken is cooked through and the cheese topping is bubbling, about 15 minutes.

CHEESY SAUSAGE ZUCCHINI CASSEROLE

Servings: 8 | Prep: 30m | Cooks: m | Total: 1h30m

NUTRITION FACTS

Calories: 305 | Carbohydrates: 17.3g | Fat: 19.6g | Protein: 15.3g | Cholesterol: 55mg

INGREDIENTS

- 1/2 cup uncooked white rice
- 4 cups cubed zucchini squash
- 1 cup water
- 2 (4 ounce) cans sliced mushrooms, drained
- 1 pound pork sausage
- 1 (8 ounce) package processed cheese food, cubed
- 1/4 cup chopped onion
- 1 pinch dried oregano
- 1 cup diced fresh tomato
- salt and pepper to taste

DIRECTIONS

1. Combine the rice and water in a small saucepan, and bring to a boil. Reduce heat to low, and simmer for about 20 minutes, or until tender. Remove from heat, and set aside.

2. Preheat the oven to 325 degrees F (165 degrees C).

3. Cook sausage and onion in a large skillet over medium heat, stirring until evenly browned. Drain excess grease. Stir in zucchini and tomatoes, and cook until tender. Stir in rice, mushrooms, and cheese. Season with oregano, salt, and pepper. Spread into a 9x13 inch baking dish, or a 2 quart casserole dish.

4. Bake, uncovered, for 1 hour in the preheated oven, or until lightly browned and bubbly.

GROUND TURKEY NOODLE BAKE

Servings: 6 | Prep: 15m | Cooks: 35m | Total: 50m

NUTRITION FACTS

Calories: 346 | Carbohydrates: 21.5g | Fat: 17.4g | Protein: 26.7g | Cholesterol: 109mg

INGREDIENTS

- 3 cups wide egg noodles
- 1/2 cup milk
- 1 pound ground turkey
- 4 ounces cream cheese
- 1 onion, chopped
- 1 tablespoon minced fresh parsley
- 1 (15 ounce) can tomato sauce
- 1 clove garlic, minced
- 1 teaspoon Italian seasoning
- 1 1/4 cups shredded part-skim mozzarella cheese

DIRECTIONS

1. Preheat oven to 375 degrees F (190 degrees C). Lightly grease an 8-inch square baking dish.
2. Bring a large pot of lightly salted water to a boil. Cook egg noodles in boiling water, stirring occasionally until cooked through but firm to the bite, about 5 minutes; drain.
3. Heat a large skillet over medium-high heat and stir in turkey and onion. Cook and stir until turkey mixture is crumbly, evenly browned, and no longer pink, about 10 minutes; drain. Stir in tomato sauce and Italian seasoning; bring to a boil. Reduce heat to low, cover, and simmer for 10 minutes.
4. Combine milk, cream cheese, parsley, and garlic in a small saucepan. Cook and stir over medium heat until cream cheese is melted, about 5 minutes.
5. Toss noodles with cream cheese mixture; transfer to prepared baking dish. Top with turkey mixture and sprinkle with mozzarella cheese.
6. Bake in preheated oven until cheese is melted, 15 to 30 minutes.

ONE POT TUNA CASSEROLE

Servings: 8 | Prep: 10m | Cooks: 20m | Total: 30m

NUTRITION FACTS

Calories: 395 | Carbohydrates: 43.2g | Fat: 17g | Protein: 17.4g | Cholesterol: 79mg

INGREDIENTS

- 1 (16 ounce) package egg noodles
- 1 (5 ounce) can tuna, drained
- 1 (10 ounce) package frozen green peas, thawed
- 1/4 cup milk
- 1/4 cup butter
- 1 cup shredded Cheddar cheese
- 1 (10.75 ounce) can condensed cream of mushroom soup

DIRECTIONS

1. Bring a large pot of lightly salted water to a boil. Cook pasta in boiling water until al dente, adding peas for the final 3 minutes of cooking; drain.
2. Melt the butter in the same pot over medium heat. Add the mushroom soup, tuna, milk, and Cheddar cheese. Stir until cheese is melted, and the mixture is smooth. Stir in the pasta and peas until evenly coated.

TATERTOT CASSEROLE

Servings: 8 | Prep: 10m | Cooks: 30m | Total: 40m

NUTRITION FACTS

Calories: 345 | Carbohydrates: 16.9g | Fat: 23.8g | Protein: 18.5g | Cholesterol: 65mg

INGREDIENTS

- 1 pound ground beef
- 2 cups shredded Cheddar cheese
- 1 pinch salt and ground black pepper to taste
- 1 (16 ounce) package frozen tater tots
- 1 (10.75 ounce) can condensed cream of mushroom soup

DIRECTIONS

1. Preheat oven to 350 degrees F (175 degrees C).
2. Cook and stir ground beef in a large skillet over medium heat until no longer pink and completely browned, 7 to 10 minutes; season with salt and black pepper. Stir cream of mushroom soup into the cooked ground beef; pour the mixture into a 9x13-inch baking dish. Layer tater tots evenly over the ground beef mixture; top with Cheddar cheese.
3. Bake until tater tots are golden brown and hot, 30 to 45 minutes.

QUICK TUNA CASSEROLE

Servings: 4 | Prep: 5m | Cooks: 20m | Total: 25m

NUTRITION FACTS

Calories: 363 | Carbohydrates: 46.1g | Fat: 7.1g | Protein: 28.1g | Cholesterol: 26mg

INGREDIENTS

- 1 (7.25 ounce) package macaroni and cheese mix
- 1 (9 ounce) can tuna, drained
- 1 (10.75 ounce) can condensed cream of mushroom soup
- 1 (10 ounce) can peas, drained

DIRECTIONS

1. Prepare macaroni and cheese mix according to package directions. Stir in the cream of mushroom soup, tuna and peas. Mix well, and heat until bubbly.

HAM, POTATO AND BROCCOLI CASSEROLE

Servings: 5 | Prep: 5m | Cooks: 40m | Total: 45m

NUTRITION FACTS

Calories: 502 | Carbohydrates: 34.7g | Fat: 31.2g | Protein: 22.8g | Cholesterol: 49mg

INGREDIENTS

- 1 (16 ounce) package frozen French fries
- 1 (10.75 ounce) can milk
- 1 (16 ounce) package frozen chopped broccoli
- 1/4 cup mayonnaise
- 1 1/2 cups cooked, cubed ham
- 1 cup grated Parmesan cheese
- 1 (10.75 ounce) can condensed cream of mushroom soup

DIRECTIONS

1. Preheat oven to 375 degrees F (190 degrees C).
2. Spray a 9x13 inch baking dish with cooking spray. Cover bottom of dish with layer of French fries. Add a layer of broccoli, then sprinkle ham evenly over broccoli. In a small bowl mix together soup, milk and mayonnaise. Pour mixture evenly over ingredients in baking dish and sprinkle with cheese.

DIFFERENT CHICKEN DIVAN

Servings: 10 | Prep: 15m | Cooks: 30m | Total: 45m

NUTRITION FACTS

Calories: 498 | Carbohydrates: 16.1g | Fat: 40.1g | Protein: 18.6g | Cholesterol: 64mg

INGREDIENTS

- 2 cups cooked, cubed chicken breast meat
- salt and pepper to taste
- 1 pound fresh broccoli, cooked and chopped
- 2 1/2 cups shredded Cheddar cheese, divided
- 1 cup mayonnaise
- 1 (10.75 ounce) can condensed cream of chicken soup
- 1 1/2 tablespoons curry powder

- 1 (10.75 ounce) can condensed cream of mushroom soup
- 1/2 teaspoon cayenne pepper
- 1 (6 ounce) can French-fried onions
- 1/2 teaspoon garlic salt

DIRECTIONS

1. Preheat oven to 350 degrees F (175 degrees C).
2. Spread chicken in the bottom of a 9x13 inch baking dish. Top with broccoli. In a medium bowl, combine the mayonnaise, curry powder, cayenne pepper, garlic salt, salt and pepper and mix well. Add 1 cup of Cheddar cheese, cream of chicken soup and cream of mushroom soup and mix again, then pour mixture over chicken and broccoli. Sprinkle with remaining 1 1/2 cups of cheese and top with onions.
3. Bake at 350 degrees F (175 degrees C) for 30 minutes.

CHICKEN, STUFFING AND GREEN BEAN CASSEROLE

Servings: 6 | Prep: 10m | Cooks: 30m | Total: 40m

NUTRITION FACTS

Calories: 426 | Carbohydrates: 48.8g | Fat: 12.7g | Protein: 27.1g | Cholesterol: 64mg

INGREDIENTS

- 2 cups cooked, cubed chicken breast meat
- salt and pepper to taste
- 1 (10.75 ounce) can condensed cream of chicken soup
- 1 (12 ounce) package unseasoned dry bread stuffing mix
- 1 (14.5 ounce) can green beans, drained
- 1 cup shredded Cheddar cheese

DIRECTIONS

1. In a medium bowl combine the chicken, soup, beans, salt and pepper; mix well and set aside. Prepare stuffing according to package directions
2. Preheat oven to 375 degrees F (190 degrees C).
3. Spoon chicken mixture into a 9x13 inch baking dish, top with prepared stuffing and sprinkle with cheese.
4. Bake, covered, for 25 minutes; remove cover and bake another 5 minutes to brown the cheese.

SPICY SAUSAGE AND RICE CASSEROLE

Servings: 6 | Prep: 20m | Cooks: 1h | Total: 1h20m

NUTRITION FACTS

Calories: 704 | Carbohydrates: 36.5g | Fat: 53.2g | Protein: 19.4g | Cholesterol: 89mg

INGREDIENTS

28 ounces fresh, ground spicy pork sausage

1 (28 ounce) can whole peeled tomatoes, crushed

1 cup uncooked long-grain rice

1 cup chicken broth

1 slice onion, diced

1 teaspoon salt

3 cloves garlic, minced

1 teaspoon ground black pepper

1 green bell pepper, chopped

1 teaspoon cayenne pepper

1 red bell pepper, chopped

1 (28 ounce) can whole peeled tomatoes, crushed

DIRECTIONS

1. Preheat oven to 350 degrees F (175 degrees C).
2. In a skillet, brown sausage and drain grease. Stir in rice, onion, garlic and peppers. Cook 5 minutes. Stir in tomatoes, chicken broth, salt, pepper and cayenne pepper. Pour into 9x13 inch pan.
3. Bake for 1 hour or until rice is tender and most of the liquid is absorbed. Or, at this step, you can cover and freeze it.

AUNT CAROL'S SPINACH AND FISH BAKE
Servings: 4 | Prep: 15m | Cooks: 20m | Total: 35m

NUTRITION FACTS

Calories: 306 | Carbohydrates: 10g | Fat: 14.3g | Protein: 34.2g | Cholesterol: 131mg

INGREDIENTS

*   1 (10 ounce) package frozen chopped spinach, thawed and squeezed dry
*   1 egg, beaten

- 1 cup sharp Cheddar cheese
- 1 pound cod fillets
- 1/3 cup dry bread crumbs
- salt and pepper to taste

DIRECTIONS

1. Preheat oven to 325 degrees F (165 degrees C).
2. In a bowl, mix the spinach, 1/2 cup Cheddar cheese, about 5 tablespoons dry bread crumbs, and the egg. Spread the mixture into the bottom of a small baking dish. Arrange the cod fillets on top of the spinach mixture, and season with salt and pepper. Top with the remaining Cheddar cheese and bread crumbs.
3. Cover, and bake 20 minutes in the preheated oven, or until fish flakes easily with a fork.

ORN DOG CASSEROLE

Servings: 12 | Prep: 15m | Cooks: 30m | Total: 45m

NUTRITION FACTS

Calories: 454 | Carbohydrates: 30.9g | Fat: 29.2g | Protein: 16.9g | Cholesterol: 88mg

INGREDIENTS

- C2 cups thinly sliced celery
- 1 1/2 cups milk
- 1 1/2 cups sliced green onions
- 2 teaspoons ground sage
- 2 tablespoons butter
- 1/4 teaspoon ground black pepper
- 1 1/2 pounds hot dogs (beef and pork frankfurters)
- 2 (8.5 ounce) packages dry corn bread mix
- 2 eggs
- 2 cups shredded Cheddar cheese, divided

DIRECTIONS

1. In a medium skillet, saute celery and green onions in butter for 5 minutes. Place saute mixture in a large bowl; set aside.
2. Slice hot dogs lengthwise into quarters, then cut into thirds. In same skillet, saute hot dogs for 5 minutes or until lightly browned. Add to celery/onion mixture and mix all together. Set aside 1 cup of mixture.
3. Preheat oven to 400 degrees F (200 degrees C).
4. In a large bowl combine the eggs, milk, sage and pepper. Add all but reserved 1 cup hot dog mixture. Stir in corn bread mix and 1 1/2 cups shredded cheese. Mix all together and spread mixture

into a shallow 3 quart baking dish. Top with reserved 1 cup hot dog mixture and remaining 1/2 cup shredded cheese.

5. Bake uncovered in preheated oven for 30 minutes, or until golden brown.

MEXICAN LASAGNA

Servings: 8 | Prep: 5m | Cooks: 45m | Total: 55m | Additional: 5m

NUTRITION FACTS

Calories: 521 | Carbohydrates: 41.8g | Fat: 22.4g | Protein: 30.8g | Cholesterol: 91mg

INGREDIENTS

- 1 pound lean ground beef
- 3 cups shredded Cheddar cheese
- 1 (1.25 ounce) package taco seasoning mix
- 2 green onions, chopped
- 2 (16 ounce) cans refried beans
- 2 roma (plum) tomatoes, chopped
- 4 (10 inch) flour tortillas

DIRECTIONS

1. Preheat oven to 375 degrees F (190 degrees C).
2. In large skillet over medium heat, cook beef until browned. Drain. Combine with taco seasoning and refried beans. Spread half of mixture in 9x13 inch baking dish. Top with two tortillas, trimming if necessary, and half of cheese. Repeat layers.
3. Bake 35 to 45 minutes until heated through and cheese is bubbly. Top with green onions and tomatoes. Let cool 5 minutes before serving.

EASY PORK CHOP CASSEROLE

Servings: 4 | Prep: 20m | Cooks: 2h | Total: 2h20m

NUTRITION FACTS

Calories: 258 | Carbohydrates: 12g | Fat: 17.7g | Protein: 12.9g | Cholesterol: 34mg

INGREDIENTS

- 1 (10.75 ounce) can condensed cream of mushroom soup
- 1 cup mushrooms, diced
- 1 packet dry onion soup mix
- 4 pork chops

- 1 (10.75 ounce) can water
- 2 tablespoons vegetable oil

DIRECTIONS

1. Preheat oven to 350 degrees F (175 degrees C).
2. In a medium bowl, combine the mushroom soup, onion soup mix, water and mushrooms.
3. In a large skillet over medium-high heat, brown the pork chops on each side. Transfer chops to a 9x9 inch baking dish, and cover with the mushroom soup mixture.
4. Bake in the preheated oven for 1 1/2 hours, or until internal pork temperature reaches 145 degrees F (63 degrees C).

COWBOY SKILLET CASSEROLE
Servings: 6 | Prep: 15m | Cooks: 20m | Total: 35m

NUTRITION FACTS

Calories: 391 | Carbohydrates: 46g | Fat: 14.2g | Protein: 21.2g | Cholesterol: 79mg

INGREDIENTS

- 1 pound ground beef
- 1 tablespoon dry fajita seasoning
- 1/2 onion, chopped
- 1 (8.5 ounce) package corn bread mix
- 2 red bell peppers, cut into 2 inch pieces
- 1 egg
- 1 (15 ounce) can baked beans
- 1/3 cup milk

DIRECTIONS

1. Preheat the oven to 350 degrees F (175 degrees C).
2. Crumble the ground beef into a large cast-iron skillet over medium-high heat. Cook, stirring frequently, until beef is evenly brown. Drain the grease, and add the onion. Cook and stir until the onion is translucent. Add the red peppers, beans, and fajita seasoning; cook and stir until heated through. Spread out in an even layer on the bottom of the skillet.
3. Mix the package of cornbread mix according to the directions using the egg and milk. Spoon over the ground beef mixture, and spread evenly.
4. Place the whole skillet in the oven, and bake for 20 minutes, or until a toothpick inserted into the cornbread layer comes out clean. Cool for a few minutes before serving.

CHEESY CHICKEN AND RICE CASSEROLE

Servings: 5 | Prep: 15m | Cooks: 30m | Total: 45m

NUTRITION FACTS

Calories: 463 | Carbohydrates: 30.3g | Fat: 20.3g | Protein: 37.3g | Cholesterol: 107mg

INGREDIENTS

- 4 skinless, boneless chicken breast halves - cut into bite size pieces
- 1 (10.75 ounce) can condensed cream of chicken soup
- salt and pepper to taste
- 2 cups shredded Cheddar cheese
- 2 cups cooked white rice
- 3 slices soft white bread, cubed

DIRECTIONS

1. Preheat oven to 350 degrees F (175 degrees C).
2. To Cook Chicken: Season chicken with salt and pepper to taste, place in a microwave-safe dish, cover and cook in microwave for 5 to 6 minutes. Turn and cook another 2 to 3 minutes or until cooked through and no longer pink inside. Let cool.
3. In a 9x13 inch baking dish, combine chicken, rice and soup and mix well. Top with cheese, then with bread cubes.
4. Bake at 350 degrees F (175 degrees C) for 20 minutes, or until cheese is melted and bubbly and bread is crunchy.

HAM AND BROCCOLI BAKE

Servings: 6 | Prep: 15m | Cooks: 45m | Total: 1h

NUTRITION FACTS

Calories: 649 | Carbohydrates: 50.9g | Fat: 39.9g | Protein: 27.6g | Cholesterol: 77mg

INGREDIENTS

- 14 ounces whole wheat rotini pasta
- 1 (15 ounce) jar Alfredo sauce
- 1 (10 ounce) package frozen broccoli
- 1/2 cup 2% milk
- 1 tablespoon olive oil
- ground black pepper to taste
- 2 cups diced fully cooked ham
- 1 cup shredded Colby-Monterey Jack cheese

DIRECTIONS

1. Preheat oven to 350 degrees F (175 degrees C). Grease a 9x13-inch baking dish.
2. Bring a large pot of lightly salted water to a boil; cook the pasta in the boiling water, stirring occasionally, until tender but not mushy, about 10 minutes. Drain.
3. Thaw the broccoli in a microwave oven until you can break it apart into small pieces.
4. Heat the olive oil in a large skillet over medium heat; cook and stir the diced ham in the hot oil until the edges start to brown, about 10 minutes. Stir in the broccoli and cook and stir until any excess water has cooked away and the ham and broccoli are hot. Pour in the jar of Alfredo sauce and the milk; stir to blend, sprinkle with pepper, and add the cooked pasta. Stir everything together to coat the pasta with sauce and bring to a simmer.
5. Spread the bubbling pasta mixture into the prepared baking dish, top with shredded Colby-Monterey jack cheese, and bake in the preheated oven until the casserole is hot and the cheese is melted and starting to brown, about 30 minutes.

SLOW COOKER TAMALE PIE

Servings: 6 | Prep: 10m | Cooks: 5h10m | Total: 5h20m

NUTRITION FACTS

Calories: 463 | Carbohydrates: 41.7g | Fat: 22g | Protein: 24.3g | Cholesterol: 99mg

INGREDIENTS

- 1 pound ground beef
- 1/3 cup milk
- 1 (15 ounce) can kidney beans, drained and rinsed
- 1 egg
- 1 (10 ounce) can enchilada sauce
- 2 tablespoons melted butter
- 1 ½ teaspoons garlic powder
- 1/2 cup shredded Cheddar cheese
- 1 (8.5 ounce) package corn bread/muffin mix

DIRECTIONS

1. Place the ground beef in a skillet over medium heat, and cook and stir the beef until it is browned, about 10 minutes, breaking up the meat as it cooks. Drain the beef, and place it into the slow cooker. Stir in the kidney beans, enchilada sauce, and garlic powder.
2. In a bowl, combine the corn bread mix with milk, egg, and butter, and stir until just mixed. Stir in the Cheddar cheese. Spoon the corn bread mixture over the beef mixture in the slow cooker.
3. Set the cooker to Low, cover, and cook until the corn bread topping is cooked through and set, about 5 hours.

TRADITIONAL STYLE VEGAN SHEPHERD'S PIE

Servings: 6 | Prep: 20m | Cooks: 55m | Total: 1h55m

NUTRITION FACTS

Calories: 552 | Carbohydrates: 64.5g | Fat: 24.4g | Protein: 20.2g | Cholesterol: 0mg

INGREDIENTS

- 5 russet potatoes, peeled and cut into 1-inch cubes
- 2 carrots, chopped
- 1/2 cup vegan mayonnaise
- 3 stalks celery, chopped
- 1/2 cup soy milk
- 1/2 cup frozen peas
- 1/4 cup olive oil
- 1 tomato, chopped
- 3 tablespoons vegan cream cheese substitute (such as Tofutti ®)
- 1 teaspoon Italian seasoning
- 2 teaspoons salt
- 1 clove garlic, minced, or more to taste
- 1 tablespoon vegetable oil
- 1 pinch ground black pepper to taste
- 1 large yellow onion, chopped
- 1 (14 ounce) package vegetarian ground beef substitute
- 1/2 cup shredded Cheddar-style soy cheese

DIRECTIONS

1. Place the potatoes in a pot, cover with cold water, and bring to a boil over medium-high heat. Turn the heat to medium-low, and boil the potatoes until tender, about 25 minutes; drain.
2. Stir the vegan mayonnaise, soy milk, olive oil, vegan cream cheese, and salt into the potatoes, and mash with a potato masher until smooth and fluffy. Set the potatoes aside.
3. Preheat oven to 400 degrees F (200 degrees C), and spray a 2-quart baking dish with cooking spray.
4. Heat the vegetable oil in a large skillet over medium heat, and cook and stir the onion, carrots, celery, frozen peas, and tomato until softened, about 10 minutes. Stir in the Italian seasoning, garlic, and pepper.
5. Reduce the heat to medium-low, and crumble the vegetarian ground beef substitute into the skillet with the vegetables. Cook and stir, breaking up the meat substitute, until the mixture is hot, about 5 minutes.
6. Spread the vegetarian meat substitute mixture into the bottom of the baking dish, and top with the mashed potatoes, smoothing them into an even layer. Sprinkle the potatoes with the shredded soy cheese.
7. Bake in the preheated oven until the cheese is melted and slightly browned and the casserole is hot, about 20 minutes.

EGG CASSEROLE

Servings: 6 | Prep: 10m | Cooks: 20m | Total: 30m

NUTRITION FACTS

Calories: 991 | Carbohydrates: 16.5g | Fat: 80.5g | Protein: 47.8g | Cholesterol: 532mg

INGREDIENTS

- 12 eggs, beaten
- 16 ounces shredded Cheddar cheese, divided
- 1 1/2 pounds ground breakfast sausage
- 7 slices white bread, torn into pieces

DIRECTIONS

1. Preheat oven to 350 degrees F (175 degrees C).
2. Brown sausage in a large skillet over medium-high heat. Drain off grease, and set aside to cool. Pour the eggs into a lightly greased 9x13 inch baking dish.
3. In a separate large bowl, combine the sausage, bread and 12 ounces of the cheese. Mix well and pour this into the egg mixture. Top with the remaining 4 ounces of cheese and cover with foil.
4. Bake at 350 degrees F (175 degrees C) for 15 minutes, uncover, and bake until casserole is golden brown and bubbly.

CHICKEN TACO CASSEROLE

Servings: 8 | Prep: 15m | Cooks: 40m | Total: 55m

NUTRITION FACTS

Calories: 508 | Carbohydrates: 31.2g | Fat: 29.4g | Protein: 32.9g | Cholesterol: 95mg

INGREDIENTS

- 4 cups shredded, cooked chicken
- 5 cups coarsely crushed tortilla chips
- 2 (10.75 ounce) cans Campbell's® Condensed Cream of Chicken Soup (Regular or 98% Fat Free)
- 2 cups shredded Cheddar cheese
- 1 cup light sour cream
- Chopped tomato
- 1 (10 ounce) can diced tomatoes and green chiles, undrained
- Sliced green onion
- 1 (15 ounce) can black beans, rinsed and drained
- Chopped fresh cilantro leaves
- 1 (1 ounce) envelope reduced-sodium taco seasoning mix

DIRECTIONS

1. Heat the oven to 350 degrees F. Lightly grease a 13x9x2-inch baking dish. Stir the chicken, soup, sour cream, tomatoes and green chiles, beans and seasoning mix in a large bowl.
2. Layer half the chicken mixture, 3 cups tortilla chips and half the cheese in the baking dish. Layer with the remaining chicken mixture and tortilla chips. Cover the baking dish.
3. Bake for 30 minutes. Uncover the baking dish. Sprinkle with the remaining cheese.
4. Bake, uncovered, for 10 minutes or until hot and bubbling and the cheese is melted. Sprinkle with the chopped tomato, green onion and cilantro before serving, if desired.

EASY MASHED POTATO AND ROASTED VEGETABLE ENCHILADAS

Servings: 12 | Prep: 40m | Cooks: 1h10m | Total: 1h50m

NUTRITION FACTS

Calories: 390 | Carbohydrates: 35.9g | Fat: 23.9g | Protein: 10.8g | Cholesterol: 54mg

INGREDIENTS

- 1 head broccoli, cut into florets
- 1 cup milk
- 8 ounces whole button mushrooms
- 1/4 cup butter
- 3 small zucchini, chopped
- 1 (7.6 ounce) package instant mashed potato flakes
- 2 cups chopped carrots
- 1 (12 ounce) package corn tortillas
- 1/4 cup olive oil
- 3 cups enchilada sauce
- salt and pepper to taste
- 8 ounces shredded Cheddar cheese
- 3 cups water

DIRECTIONS

1. Preheat oven to 425 degrees F (220 degrees C).
2. In a large mixing bowl, combine broccoli, mushrooms, zucchini, and carrots. Drizzle the vegetables with olive oil, and season with salt and pepper. Spread vegetables in a single layer in a shallow baking dish. Roast vegetables in the preheated oven for 30 to 40 minutes; stir halfway through their cooking time. When finished cooking, remove from the oven, and reduce oven temperature to 350 degrees F (175 degrees C).

3. Bring water, milk, and butter to a boil in a large pot. Remove the pot from heat, and mix in the mashed potato flakes. Let stand two minutes, then stir the mashed potatoes with a fork until they are smooth. Stir in roasted vegetables.
4. In a dry, nonstick skillet over medium heat, quickly heat each tortilla on both sides to make pliable. Dip the tortillas in enchilada sauce. Put a large spoonful (approximately 1/4 to 1/3 cup) of potato-veggie mixture into the center of each tortilla. Top mixture with about 1 to 2 tablespoons cheese, and roll tortillas. Place seam-side down in a 9x13 inch baking dish. Pour extra sauce over top, and sprinkle with remaining cheese.
5. Bake at 350 degrees F (175 degrees C) for approximately 20 to 30 minutes, or until the enchiladas are heated through.

THANKSGIVING LEFTOVER CASSEROLE
Servings: 8 | Prep: 20m | Cooks: 55m | Total: 1h15m

NUTRITION FACTS

Calories: 377 | Carbohydrates: 34.4g | Fat: 19.4g | Protein: 15.9g | Cholesterol: 67mg

INGREDIENTS

- 3 tablespoons butter
- 1/4 teaspoon onion powder
- 2 tablespoons all-purpose flour
- 2 tablespoons butter
- 1 (12 fluid ounce) can evaporated milk
- 1 cup finely crushed herb-seasoned dry bread stuffing mix
- 1 cup water
- 1 cup cooked, diced turkey meat
- 1/4 teaspoon salt
- 1 cup shredded Cheddar cheese
- 1/4 teaspoon freshly ground black pepper
- 2 cups leftover mashed potatoes

DIRECTIONS

1. Preheat oven to 350 degrees F (175 degrees C). Lightly grease a 9x13 inch baking dish.
2. Melt 3 tablespoons butter in a saucepan over low heat. Blend in the flour. Slowly stir in evaporated milk and water, then season with salt, pepper, and onion powder. Stir sauce over low heat for 5 minutes.
3. In a separate saucepan over low heat, melt 2 tablespoons butter. Blend in the dry stuffing mix. Place the turkey in the prepared baking dish. Pour the sauce over turkey, then sprinkle with Cheddar cheese. Spread mashed potatoes over cheese. Top mashed potatoes with the stuffing mixture.
4. Bake 45 minutes in the preheated oven.

TATER TOT CASSEROLE

Servings: 4 | Prep: 15m | Cooks: 30m | Total: 45m

NUTRITION FACTS

Calories: 404 | Carbohydrates: 40.7g | Fat: 21.9g | Protein: 17g | Cholesterol: 36mg

INGREDIENTS

- 1/2 pound ground beef
- 1 teaspoon garlic salt
- 1 (10.75 ounce) can condensed cream of mushroom soup
- 1 (14.5 ounce) can French style green beans
- 10 3/4 fluid ounces skim milk
- 1/2 (32 ounce) package tater tots

DIRECTIONS

1. Preheat oven to 375 degrees F (190 degrees C).
2. In a large skillet over high heat, brown the ground beef and drain fat. Stir in condensed cream of mushroom soup, skim milk, garlic salt and green beans. Pour the mixture into a medium-sized casserole dish and layer with the tater tots.
3. Bake in preheated oven for about 30 minutes, or until tater tots are browned and crispy.

EASY BBQ BAKE

Servings: 4 | Prep: 15m | Cooks: 45m | Total: 1h

NUTRITION FACTS

Calories: 433 | Carbohydrates: 79.5g | Fat: 1.7g | Protein: 28.3g | Cholesterol: 68mg

INGREDIENTS

- 3/4 cup barbecue sauce
- 1 onion, chopped
- 3/4 cup honey
- 4 skinless, boneless chicken breast halves
- 1/2 cup ketchup

DIRECTIONS

1. Preheat oven to 400 degrees F (200 degrees C).
2. In a medium bowl, combine the barbecue sauce, honey, ketchup and onion and mix well. Place chicken in a 9x13 inch baking dish. Pour sauce over the chicken and cover dish with foil.
3. Bake at 400 degrees F (200 degrees C) for 45 minutes to 1 hour, or until chicken juices run clear.

HEARTY TUNA CASSEROLE

Servings: 6 | Prep: 15m | Cooks: 45m | Total: 1h

NUTRITION FACTS

Calories: 356 | Carbohydrates: 15.7g | Fat: 24.5g | Protein: 18.8g | Cholesterol: 56mg

INGREDIENTS

- 3 cups uncooked egg noodles
- 1/2 cup mayonnaise
- 2 (5 ounce) cans tuna, drained
- 1/2 teaspoon dried thyme
- 1/2 cup chopped celery
- 1/4 teaspoon salt
- 1/3 cup chopped green onions
- 1 small zucchini, sliced
- 1/3 cup sour cream
- 1 cup shredded Monterey Jack cheese
- 2 teaspoons prepared mustard
- 1 tomato, chopped

DIRECTIONS

1. Preheat oven to 350 degrees F (175 degrees C). Grease a 2 quart casserole dish.
2. Bring a large pot of salted water to a boil, add noodles, and cook until al dente; drain.
3. In a large mixing bowl, combine noodles, tuna, celery, and green onion. Stir in sour cream, mustard, and mayonnaise. Season with salt and thyme. Spoon 1/2 of the noodle mixture into the prepared casserole dish. Arrange a layer of zucchini over the mixture. Top with the remaining noodles, followed by a layer of zucchini. Top the entire casserole with cheese.
4. Bake in preheated oven for 30 minutes, or until hot and bubbly. Sprinkle the casserole with tomatoes before serving.

MEXICAN CASSEROLE

Servings: 4 | Prep: 10m | Cooks: 20m | Total: 30m

NUTRITION FACTS

Calories: 651 | Carbohydrates: 74g | Fat: 20.3g | Protein: 29.3g | Cholesterol: 68mg

INGREDIENTS

- 1 (16 ounce) can refried beans
- 1 cup salsa
- 3/4 onion, diced

- 2 cups shredded Cheddar or Colby Jack cheese
- 5 (10 inch) flour tortillas

DIRECTIONS

1. Preheat oven to 375 degrees F (190 degrees C). Spray a 9-inch pie pan with non-stick cooking spray.
2. In a saucepan, cook refried beans and onions (to soften them) on medium-high heat for about 5 minutes.
3. Place one tortilla in the bottom of the greased pan. Spread about 1/3 cup of the bean mixture over it. Layer a few tablespoons of salsa over this. Then, place another tortilla over the salsa, and add more of the bean mixture. Follow the beans with a big handful of cheese, spreading evenly. repeat layers, spreading the ingredients evenly over the tortillas. On the top layer, make sure to use lots of salsa and cheese!
4. Bake until the cheese is melted, approximately 15 to 20 minutes.

POPPY SEED CHICKEN CASSEROLE

Servings: 6 | Prep: 20m | Cooks: 50m | Total: 1h10m

NUTRITION FACTS

Calories: 593 | Carbohydrates: 16.9g | Fat: 45.7g | Protein: 28.4g | Cholesterol: 142mg

INGREDIENTS

- 4 skinless, boneless chicken breast halves
- 1 (8 ounce) container sour cream
- 1/2 cup butter, melted
- 1 (10.75 ounce) can condensed cream of chicken soup
- 1 sleeve buttery round crackers (such as Ritz®), crushed
- 2 cups shredded Cheddar cheese
- 1 teaspoon poppy seeds, or more if desired

DIRECTIONS

1. Place the chicken breasts into a large pot and cover with water. Bring to a boil over high heat, then reduce heat to medium, cover, and simmer until the chicken breasts are no longer pink in the center, about 20 minutes. Drain the water, then shred the chicken.
2. Preheat an oven to 350 degrees F (175 degrees C). Combine the butter, crackers, and poppy seeds in a bowl; set aside.
3. Blend the sour cream and cream of chicken soup in a bowl; pour half of the soup mixture into a 9x9-inch baking dish. Add the shredded chicken, then pour the remaining half of the soup mixture on top. Sprinkle with Cheddar cheese, then top with the cracker mixture.
4. Bake in the preheated oven until cheese has melted and the sauce is bubbly, 25 to 30 minutes.

TUNA NOODLE CASSEROLE

Servings: 4 | Prep: 5m | Cooks: 30m | Total: 35m

NUTRITION FACTS

Calories: 551 | Carbohydrates: 50.4g | Fat: 28g | Protein: 24.5g | Cholesterol: 114mg

INGREDIENTS

- 1 (8 ounce) package wide egg noodles
- 1 (5 ounce) can tuna, drained
- 1/4 cup butter, cubed
- 1 (10.75 ounce) can condensed cream of mushroom soup
- 4 slices American cheese
- 1/4 cup bread crumbs

DIRECTIONS

1. Preheat oven to 350 degrees F (175 degrees C). Bring a large pot of lightly salted water to a boil. Add pasta and cook for 8 to 10 minutes or until al dente; drain.
2. In a 1 1/2 quart glass casserole dish, layer noodles, butter cubes, 2 slices of cheese, 1/2 of the tuna, and 1/2 of the soup. Repeat the layering with the remaining ingredients. Top the casserole with bread crumbs.
3. Bake at 350 degrees F (175 degrees C) for 10 to 15 minutes.

TACO BAKE

Servings: 8 | Prep: 25m | Cooks: 20m | Total: 45m

NUTRITION FACTS

Calories: 663 | Carbohydrates: 48.3g | Fat: 40.2g | Protein: 28.6g | Cholesterol: 95mg

INGREDIENTS

- 1 1/2 pounds lean ground beef
- 1 (1.25 ounce) package taco seasoning mix
- 1 (14.5 ounce) can diced tomatoes with green chile peppers, drained
- 8 ounces shredded Colby-Monterey Jack cheese
- 1/2 cup water
- 1 (18 ounce) package corn tortilla chips
- 1 cup sour cream

DIRECTIONS

1. Preheat oven to 350 degrees F (175 degrees C).

2. In a medium skillet over medium heat, brown the ground beef and drain fat. Add the diced tomatoes with green chile peppers, water, sour cream and taco seasoning mix. Let simmer for 5 to 10 minutes.
3. In the bottom of a 9x13 inch baking dish, place a layer of tortilla chips. Cover with a layer of the meat mixture then a layer of cheese. Repeat this process until the last layer is cheese.
4. Bake in the preheated oven for 20 minutes, or until the cheese is bubbly.

SOUTHERN GRITS CASSEROLE
Servings: 16 | Prep: 15m | Cooks: 45m | Total: 1h

NUTRITION FACTS

Calories: 403 | Carbohydrates: 16.8g | Fat: 29.9g | Protein: 16.5g | Cholesterol: 202mg

INGREDIENTS

- 6 cups water
- 1 pound ground pork sausage
- 2 cups uncooked grits
- 12 eggs
- 1/2 cup butter, divided
- 1/2 cup milk
- 3 cups shredded Cheddar cheese, divided

DIRECTIONS

1. Preheat oven to 350 degrees F (175 degrees C). Lightly grease a large baking dish.
2. Bring water to a boil in a large saucepan, and stir in grits. Reduce heat, cover, and simmer about 5 minutes, until liquid has been absorbed. Mix in 1/2 the butter and 2 cups cheese until melted.
3. In a skillet over medium-high heat, cook the sausage until evenly browned. Drain, and mix into the grits. Beat together the eggs and milk in a bowl, and pour into the skillet. Lightly scramble, then mix into the grits.
4. Pour the grits mixture into the prepared baking dish. Dot with remaining butter, and top with remaining cheese. Season with salt and pepper.
5. Bake 30 minutes in the preheated oven, until lightly browned.

CHEESE LOVER'S TUNA CASSEROLE
Servings: 6 | Prep: 5m | Cooks: 25m | Total: 30m

NUTRITION FACTS

Calories: 508 | Carbohydrates: 23.8g | Fat: 30.5g | Protein: 33.7g | Cholesterol: 93mg

INGREDIENTS

- 1 cup elbow macaroni
- 1 pound Cheddar cheese, cubed
- 1 (10.75 ounce) can condensed cream of mushroom soup
- 1 1/2 cups seasoned croutons
- 2 (5 ounce) cans tuna, drained

DIRECTIONS

1. Preheat oven to 350 degrees F (175 degrees C).
2. Bring a large pot of lightly salted water to a boil. Add pasta and cook for 8 to 10 minutes or until al dente; drain. Meanwhile, in a 9x13 inch baking dish, combine soup, tuna and 1/2 of the cheese; mix well.
3. Add pasta to baking dish and mix together. Add remaining cheese to the top of the mixture, then add croutons. Cover dish and bake in preheated oven for 15 minutes or until the cheese is melted; serve.

BIEROCK CASSEROLE

Servings: 6 | Prep: 20m | Cooks: 25m | Total: 45m

NUTRITION FACTS

Calories: 674 | Carbohydrates: 32.5g | Fat: 42.3g | Protein: 37.1g | Cholesterol: 114mg

INGREDIENTS

- 1/2 cup chopped onion
- 2 (8 ounce) cans refrigerated crescent rolls
- 1 1/2 pounds lean ground beef
- 1 (8 ounce) package shredded Cheddar cheese
- 1 (16 ounce) can sauerkraut, drained and pressed dry

DIRECTIONS

1. Preheat oven to 350 degrees F (175 degrees C).
2. Brown onion and ground beef in a large skillet over medium high heat; drain extra fat out of skillet, then stir in drained sauerkraut. Heat through and set aside.
3. Press 1 package of crescent roll dough into the bottom of a lightly greased 9x13 inch baking dish. Spread beef mixture on top, then lay 2nd package of crescent roll dough over the top of the beef mixture. Press dough seams together and sprinkle all with cheese.
4. Bake in preheated oven for 25 to 30 minutes, or until golden brown.

GREEN CHICKEN ENCHILADA

Servings: 6 | Prep: 15m | Cooks: 1h | Total: 1h15m

NUTRITION FACTS

Calories: 724 | Carbohydrates: 77.2g | Fat: 29.2g | Protein: 36.8g | Cholesterol: 89mg

INGREDIENTS

- 1 pound skinless, boneless chicken breast halves
- 1 (8 ounce) package shredded Monterey Jack cheese
- 12 (10 inch) flour tortillas
- 1 (19 ounce) can green enchilada sauce

DIRECTIONS

1. In a pot with enough water to cover, boil the chicken 25 minutes, or until juices run clear. Drain, cool, and shred.
2. Preheat oven to 350 degrees F (175 degrees C). Lightly grease a medium baking dish.
3. Fill each tortilla with equal amounts of chicken and cheese, reserving 1/4 cup cheese for topping. Roll tortillas to form enchiladas. Arrange enchiladas in the prepared baking dish. Cover with the enchilada sauce.
4. Bake enchiladas 30 minutes in the preheated oven. Top with reserved cheese, and continue baking 5 minutes, until cheese is melted.

ENCHILADA CASSEROLE

Servings: 8 | Prep: 15m | Cooks: 45m | Total: 1h

NUTRITION FACTS

Calories: 375 | Carbohydrates: 24.9g | Fat: 24g | Protein: 17.4g | Cholesterol: 54mg

INGREDIENTS

- 1 (15 ounce) can black beans, rinsed and drained
- 1 (8 ounce) package tempeh, crumbled
- 2 cloves garlic, minced
- 6 (6 inch) corn tortillas
- 1 onion, chopped
- 1 (19 ounce) can enchilada sauce
- 1 (4 ounce) can diced green chile peppers
- 1 (6 ounce) can sliced black olives
- 1 jalapeno pepper, seeded and minced
- 8 ounces shredded Cheddar cheese

DIRECTIONS

1. Preheat oven to 350 degrees (175 degrees C). Lightly oil a 9x13 inch baking dish.

2. In a medium bowl, combine the beans, garlic, onion, chile peppers, jalapeno pepper, and tempeh. Pour enchilada sauce into a shallow bowl.
3. Dip three tortillas in the enchilada sauce, and place them in the prepared baking dish. Be sure to cover the bottom of the dish as completely as possible. Place 1/2 of the bean mixture on top of the tortillas, and repeat. Drizzle the remaining sauce over the casserole, and sprinkle with olives and shredded cheese.
4. Cover, and bake for 30 minutes. Uncover, and continue baking for an additional 15 minutes, or until the casserole is bubbling and the cheese is melted.

CHEESY PORK CHOP CASSEROLE
Servings: 4 | Prep: 15m | Cooks: 1h | Total: 1h15m

NUTRITION FACTS

Calories: 559 | Carbohydrates: 27.6g | Fat: 29.8g | Protein: 44.9g | Cholesterol: 135mg

INGREDIENTS

- 4 potatoes, peeled and sliced
- 1 (10.5 ounce) can condensed French onion soup
- 4 thick cut boneless pork chops
- 1 (8 ounce) package shredded Monterey Jack chees
- 1 (10.75 ounce) can condensed Cheddar cheese soup

DIRECTIONS

1. Preheat oven to 350 degrees F (175 degrees C).
2. Line the bottom of a 9x13 inch baking pan with sliced potatoes. Arrange the pork chops on top of the potatoes.
3. In a bowl, stir together the cheddar cheese and French onion soups. Pour the soup over the pork chops.
4. Cover pan and bake in preheated oven for 60 minutes, or until internal pork temperature reaches 145 degrees F (63 degrees C). Sprinkle chops with Monterey Jack cheese and serve.

SPAGHETTI SQUASH CASSEROLE IN THE SHELL
Servings: 6 | Prep: 25m | Cooks: 1h19m | Total: 1h51m | Additional: 7m

NUTRITION FACTS

Calories: 236 | Carbohydrates: 12.8g | Fat: g | Protein: 18g | Cholesterol: 58mg

INGREDIENTS

- 1 spaghetti squash, halved and seeded

* 1 teaspoon dried oregano
* 1 pound lean ground beef
* 1/2 teaspoon salt
* 1/2 cup finely chopped onion
* 1/4 teaspoon ground black pepper
* 1/2 cup minced bell pepper
* 1 (14.5 ounce) can diced tomatoes, drained
* 1 clove garlic, minced
* 1/3 cup shredded Cheddar cheese
* 1 teaspoon dried basil

DIRECTIONS

1. Preheat oven to 375 degrees F (190 degrees C). Place squash in baking pan; pour in enough boiling water to come 1/2-inch up the sides of dish.
2. Bake in the preheated oven until squash is tender, 40 to 45 minutes. Remove from oven; cool until easily handled, 7 to 10 minutes.
3. Reduce oven to 350 degrees F (175 degrees C). Scoop out squash; separate strands with a fork. Reserve shells.
4. Cook beef, onion, and bell pepper in a skillet over medium heat until the meat is no longer pink, about 5 minutes; drain. Stir in garlic, basil, oregano, salt, and pepper; cook and stir until fragrant, about 2 minutes. Add tomatoes and cook until warmed through, about 2 minutes. Stir in squash; cook until liquid has evaporated, about 10 minutes.
5. Fill squash shells with squash mixture using a slotted spoon; place in a shallow baking pan.
6. Bake in the preheated oven until flavors combine, about 15 minutes. Sprinkle with Cheddar cheese; bake until cheese is melted, about 5 minutes.

SPAGHETTI PIZZA

Servings: 7 | Prep: 20m | Cooks: 45m | Total: 1h10m | Additional: 5m

NUTRITION FACTS

Calories: 351 | Carbohydrates: 34.2g | Fat: 15.3g | Protein: 18g | Cholesterol: 66mg

INGREDIENTS

* 1 (8 ounce) package spaghetti, broken into 2-inch pieces
* 1/4 teaspoon garlic salt
* 1 egg, beaten
* 1 (16 ounce) jar spaghetti sauce
* 1/4 cup milk
* 1 teaspoon dried oregano
* 2 cups shredded mozzarella cheese, divided

- 1/4 teaspoon dried basil
- 1/4 teaspoon salt
- 4 ounces pepperoni sausage, sliced

DIRECTIONS

1. Preheat oven to 425 degrees F (220 degrees C). Grease a 9x13-inch baking dish.
2. Bring a large pot of lightly salted water to a boil. Add spaghetti and cook for 8 to 10 minutes or until al dente; drain and rinse with cold water.
3. Combine egg, milk, 1/2 cup of the mozzarella cheese, salt, and garlic salt in a large bowl. Stir in cooked spaghetti; mix well.
4. Spread mixture into prepared baking dish. Bake in preheated oven for 15 minutes. Remove from oven and reduce temperature to 350 degrees F (175 degrees C).
5. Spread sauce over spaghetti. Sprinkle with oregano, basil, and the remaining 1 1/2 cups mozzarella. Top with pepperoni, return to oven, and bake until cheese is bubbly and beginning to brown, about 30 minutes more. Let stand 5 minutes before cutting.

FRESH ASPARAGUS AND CHICKEN CASSEROLE

Servings: 6 | Prep: 30m | Cooks: 45m | Total: 1h15m

NUTRITION FACTS

Calories: 376 | Carbohydrates: 32.7g | Fat: 20.1g | Protein: 17.3g | Cholesterol: 77mg

INGREDIENTS

- 1 (8 ounce) package egg noodles
- 1 cup chicken stock
- 1 1/3 tablespoons olive oil
- 1 1/2 cups sour cream
- 1 onion, chopped
- 1/2 teaspoon dried oregano
- 1 cup chopped, cooked chicken meat
- 1 pound fresh asparagus, trimmed and cut into 2 inch pieces
- 1 red bell pepper, chopped
- 8 tablespoons grated Parmesan cheese, divided
- 2 stalks celery, chopped

DIRECTIONS

1. Preheat oven to 350 degrees F (175 degrees C). Lightly grease a 1 1/2 quart casserole dish.
2. Cook noodles in a large pot of boiling water for 5 minutes, or until almost tender. Drain, and rinse under cold water.

3. Heat the olive oil in a heavy skillet over medium heat. Cook onion for 4 to 5 minutes, stirring frequently. Add chicken, red bell pepper, celery, and chicken stock. Bring to a boil, and simmer for 5 minutes. Stir in sour cream and oregano.
4. Spread half of the chicken mixture into the prepared dish. Arrange the asparagus over the chicken, spread cooked noodles evenly over the asparagus, and top with 5 tablespoons of Parmesan cheese. Cover with the remaining chicken mixture. Sprinkle with the reserved Parmesan cheese.
5. Bake 30 minutes in the preheated oven, until lightly brown.

EASY CHEAP AND YUMMY CASSEROLE

Servings: 8 | Prep: 15m | Cooks: 45m | Total: 1h

NUTRITION FACTS

Calories: 565 | Carbohydrates: 43g | Fat: 36.1g | Protein: 19.4g | Cholesterol: 60mg

INGREDIENTS

- 1 (28 ounce) can baked beans
- 1 (7.5 ounce) package corn bread mix
- 2 (16 ounce) packages hot dogs, sliced

DIRECTIONS

1. Preheat the oven to 400 degrees F (200 degrees C).
2. Pour the can of beans into a 9x13 inch baking dish so they cover the bottom. Arrange hot dog slices so they cover the beans as completely as possible. If too much juice seeps through to the cornbread, it will take longer to cook. Prepare cornbread mix according to package directions. Spread the batter evenly over the hot dog layer.
3. Bake for 35 to 40 minutes, or until cornbread is cooked through. A toothpick inserted into the center should come out clean.

HAM AND SWISS CASSEROLE

Servings: 4 | Prep: 15m | Cooks: 30m | Total: 45m

NUTRITION FACTS

Calories: 432 | Carbohydrates: 21g | Fat: 28g | Protein: 24.7g | Cholesterol: 163mg

INGREDIENTS

- 2 cups egg noodles
- 1 teaspoon salt
- 2 tablespoons vegetable oil

- 1/2 teaspoon ground black pepper
- 1 cup chopped onions
- 2 eggs
- 1 (6 ounce) can mushrooms, drained
- 1/4 cup milk
- 1 cup diced cooked ham
- 1/4 cup grated Parmesan cheese
- 1 cup diced Swiss cheese

DIRECTIONS

1. Bring a large pot of lightly salted water to a boil. Add egg noodles and cook for 8 to 10 minutes or until al dente; drain.
2. Preheat oven to 400 degrees F (200 degrees C).
3. Toss drained noodles with 2 teaspoons of the oil. Heat remaining oil in a skillet and saute onion over medium heat until soft. Combine noodles, onion, mushrooms, ham, Swiss cheese, salt and pepper. Transfer to a greased 3 quart casserole dish. In a bowl mix together egg and milk; pour over noodle mixture. Sprinkle with parmesan cheese.
4. Bake in a preheated oven for 30 minutes.

TOMMY'S HAM CASSEROLE

Servings: 6 | Prep: 15m | Cooks: 30m | Total: 45m

NUTRITION FACTS

Calories: 328 | Carbohydrates: 29.9g | Fat: 13.4g | Protein: 20.7g | Cholesterol: 46mg

INGREDIENTS

- 2 cups cubed or shredded ham
- 1 (10.75 ounce) can condensed cream of mushroom soup
- 3 cups cooked macaroni
- 1/2 (10.75 ounce) can milk
- 3/4 cup shredded Cheddar cheese
- 1/4 cup dried bread crumbs

DIRECTIONS

1. Preheat oven to 375 degrees F (190 degrees C).
2. In a casserole dish, combine the ham, macaroni, cheese, soup and milk. Mix together well.
3. Bake, covered, at 375 degrees F (190 degrees C) for 20 minutes. Uncover, top with the bread crumbs, and bake, uncovered for 10 more minutes.

CHICKEN CORDON BLEU CASSEROLE

Servings: 8 | Prep: 15m | Cooks: 40m | Total: 55m

NUTRITION FACTS

Calories: 500 | Carbohydrates: 24.2g | Fat: 28g | Protein: 36.2g | Cholesterol: 137mg

INGREDIENTS

- 1 egg
- 8 ounces Swiss cheese, cubed
- 1/2 cup milk
- 8 ounces cubed ham
- 2 pounds skinless, boneless chicken breast halves - cut into chunks
- 1 (10.75 ounce) can condensed cream of chicken soup
- 1 cup plain dried bread crumbs
- 1 cup milk
- 1 cup oil for frying

DIRECTIONS

1. Preheat oven to 350 degrees F (175 degrees C).
2. Beat egg and 1/2 cup milk together until combined. Stir in the chicken chunks to coat, then drain, and coat with bread crumbs. Heat oil in a large skillet to 375 degrees F (190 degrees C). Fry breaded chicken cubes in hot oil until golden brown on all sides, then remove, and drain on paper towels.
3. Place chicken cubes in a glass baking dish, along with the Swiss cheese, and ham. Stir together the soup with 1 cup milk, pour over casserole.
4. Bake in preheated oven until golden brown and bubbly, about 30 minutes.

TATER TOT HOT DISH

Servings: 6 | Prep: 10m | Cooks: 1h | Total: 1h10m

NUTRITION FACTS

Calories: 744 | Carbohydrates: 59.6g | Fat: 47.7g | Protein: 25.4g | Cholesterol: 68mg

INGREDIENTS

- 1 1/2 pounds lean ground beef
- 1 (32 ounce) package tater tots, thawed
- 1 onion, chopped
- 1 (10.75 ounce) can condensed cream of mushroom soup
- 3/4 teaspoon salt
- 1 (10.75 ounce) can condensed cream of celery soup

- 1 pinch ground black pepper
- 1 (6 ounce) can French-fried onion rings

DIRECTIONS

1. Preheat oven to 350 degrees F (175 degrees C).
2. In a large skillet cook ground beef with onion, salt and pepper; drain and spread into the bottom of a 9x13 inch baking dish. Add tater tots; mix cream of mushroom and cream of celery soup together and pour mixture over dish. Top with onion rings, if using.
3. Bake in preheated oven for 1 hour.

CREAMY TATER TOT CASSEROLE

Servings: 8 | Prep: 15m | Cooks: 1h | Total: 1h15m

NUTRITION FACTS

Calories: 707 | Carbohydrates: 44.9g | Fat: 56.3g | Protein: 14.2g | Cholesterol: 119mg

INGREDIENTS

- 2 pounds tater tots, thawed
- 1/2 teaspoon seasoning salt
- 1 (10.5 ounce) can condensed cream of chicken soup
- 1/2 cup butter, softened
- 1 cup finely chopped onion
- 3 cups cornflakes cereal
- 1 (16 ounce) container sour cream
- 1/2 cup butter, melted
- 1 (8 ounce) package sharp Cheddar cheese, shredded
- 2 tablespoons grated Parmesan cheese
- 1 dash garlic powder
- paprika to taste

DIRECTIONS

1. Preheat oven to 350 degrees F (175 degrees C). Grease a 9x13 inch casserole dish.
2. In a large mixing bowl combine tater tots, soup, onion, sour cream, cheese, garlic powder, seasoning salt and softened butter; mix well. Transfer to casserole dish. In a medium bowl combine cereal and melted butter; spread over casserole. Sprinkle the top with parmesan cheese (use more or less according to your taste) and paprika.
3. Bake in preheated oven for 45 minutes to 1 hour, or until browned. (Note: It's a good idea to put a cookie sheet under the casserole dish, in case it bubbles over while cooking.)

SILVER'S SAVORY CHICKEN AND BROCCOLI CASSEROLE

Servings: 6 | Prep: 20m | Cooks: 20m | Total: 40m

NUTRITION FACTS

Calories: 580 | Carbohydrates: 30.1g | Fat: 28.6g | Protein: 49.4g | Cholesterol: 164mg

INGREDIENTS

- 6 ounces egg noodles
- salt and pepper to taste
- 3 tablespoons butter
- 5 cups cooked, shredded chicken breast meat
- 1 yellow onion, chopped
- 1 (10 ounce) package chopped frozen broccoli, thawed
- 1/4 cup all-purpose flour
- 1 cup shredded Cheddar cheese
- 1 1/2 cups chicken broth
- 1 cup shredded provolone cheese
- 3/4 cup milk

DIRECTIONS

1. Bring a large pot of lightly salted water to a boil. Add pasta and cook for 6 to 8 minutes or until al dente; drain. Preheat oven to 400 degrees F (200 degrees C.) Grease a 9x13 inch casserole dish.
2. Melt butter in a large saucepan over medium heat. Saute onion until tender, about 3 minutes. Mix in flour. Gradually stir in chicken broth. Slowly stir in milk, and cook, stirring, until sauce begins to thicken. Season with salt and pepper.
3. Place cooked noodles in the bottom of casserole dish. Arrange cooked chicken in an even layer over noodles. Place broccoli over the chicken. Pour sauce evenly over the broccoli. Combine cheeses, and sprinkle half over the casserole.
4. Bake in preheated oven for 20 minutes, or until the cheese melts. Remove from oven, and sprinkle with remaining cheese. Allow to set for 5 minutes, until cheese melts.Sm low heat, and whisk in flour.